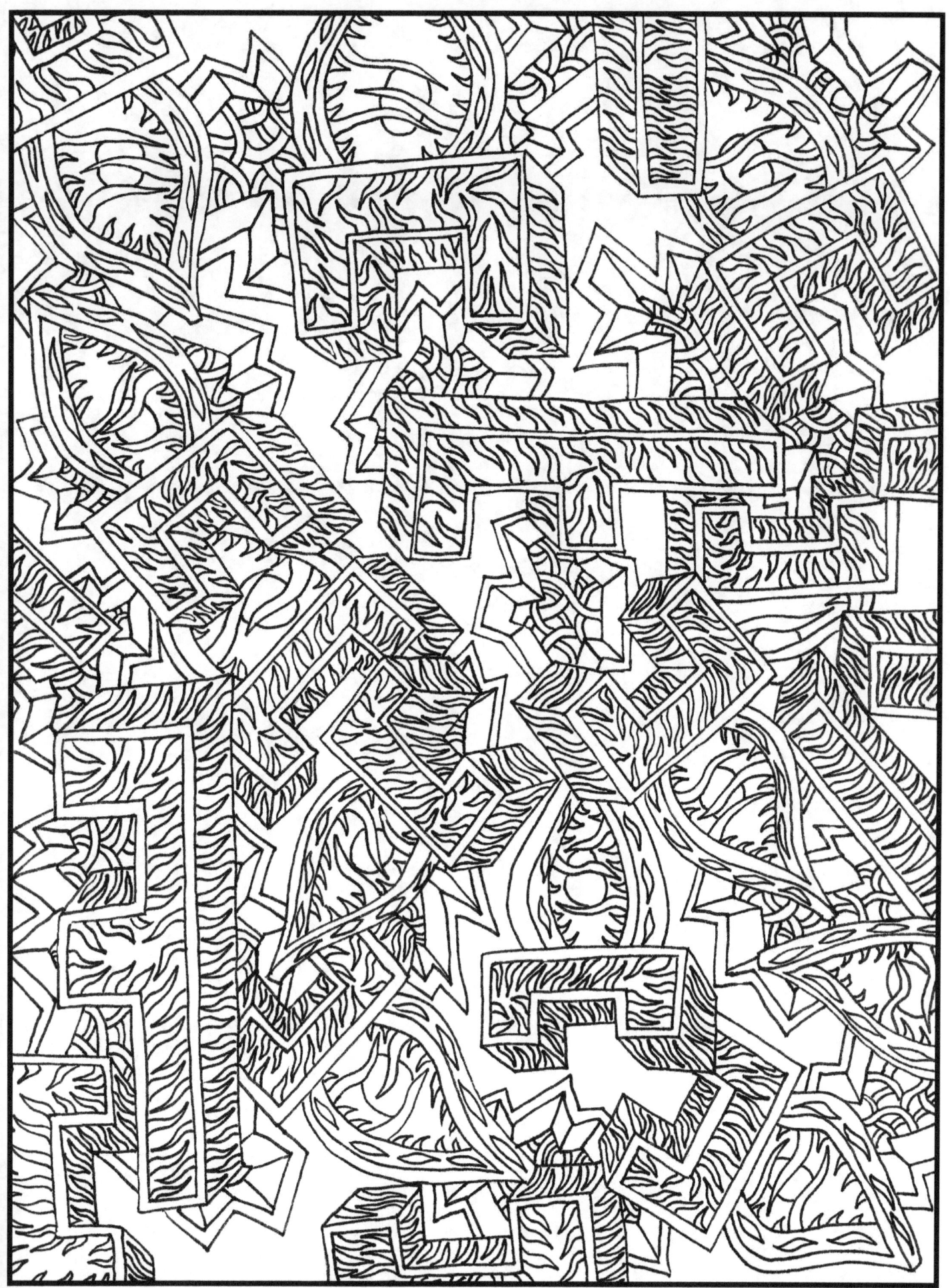

© Damone Heins

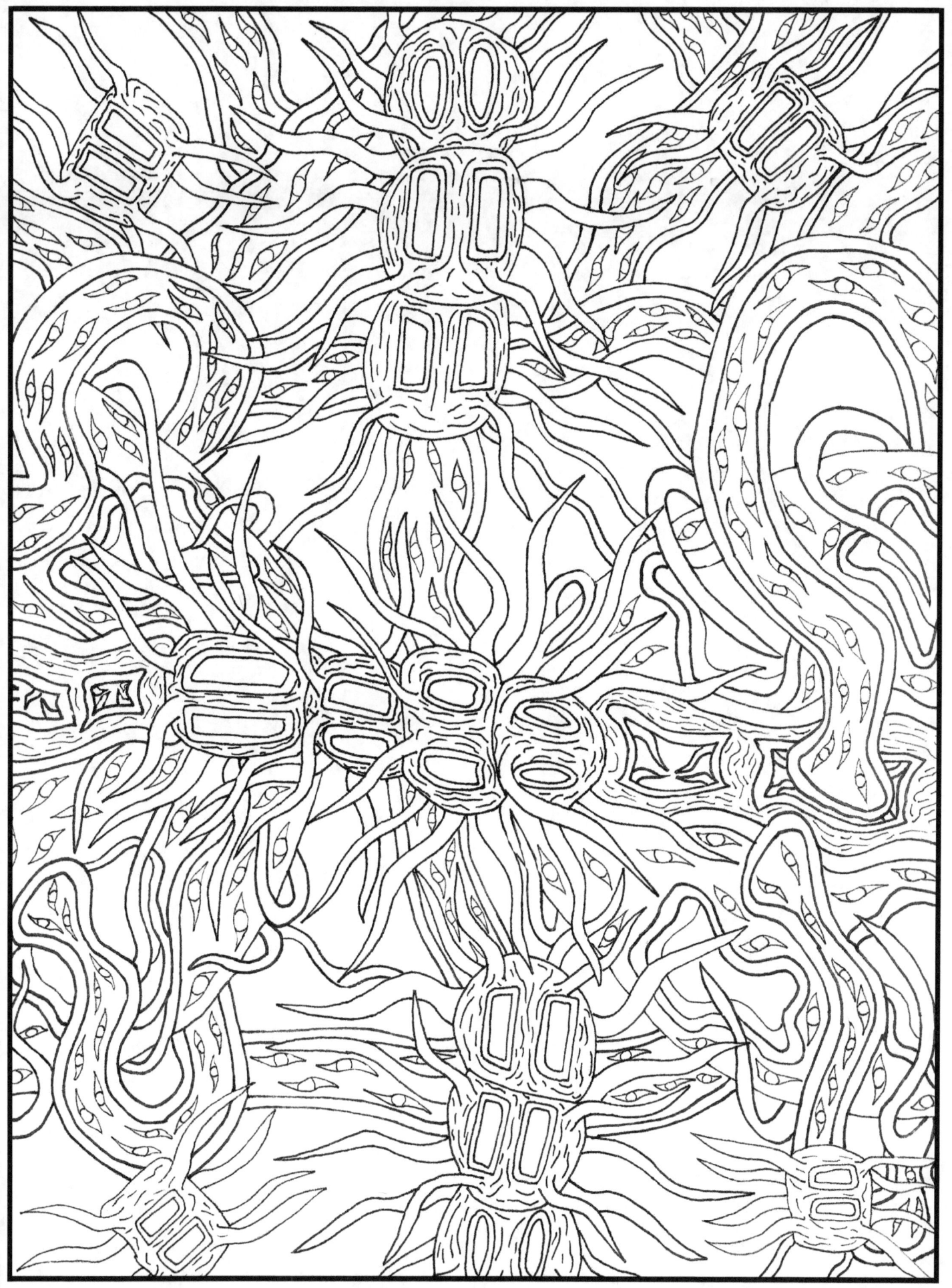

© Damone Heins

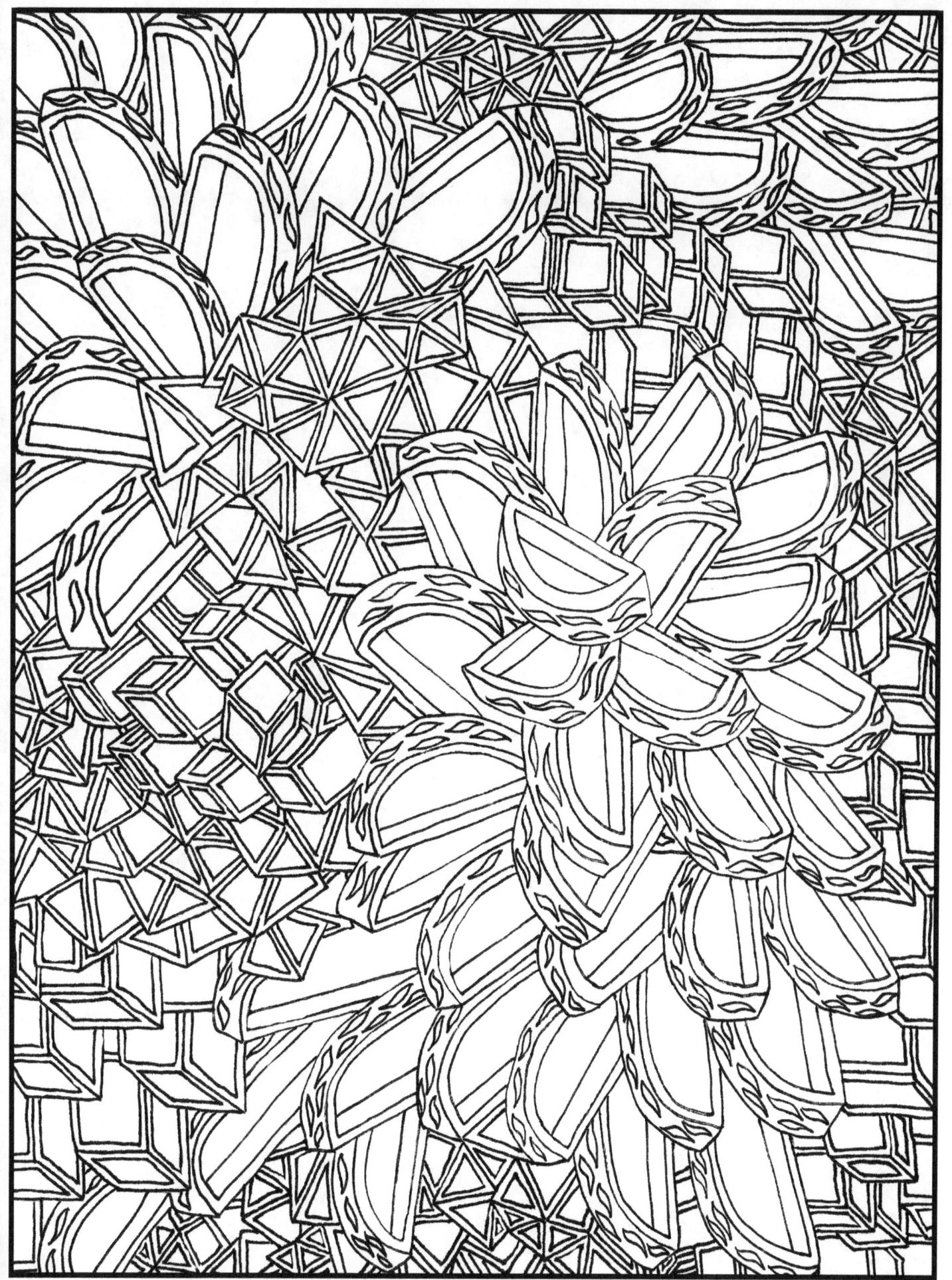

© Damone Heins

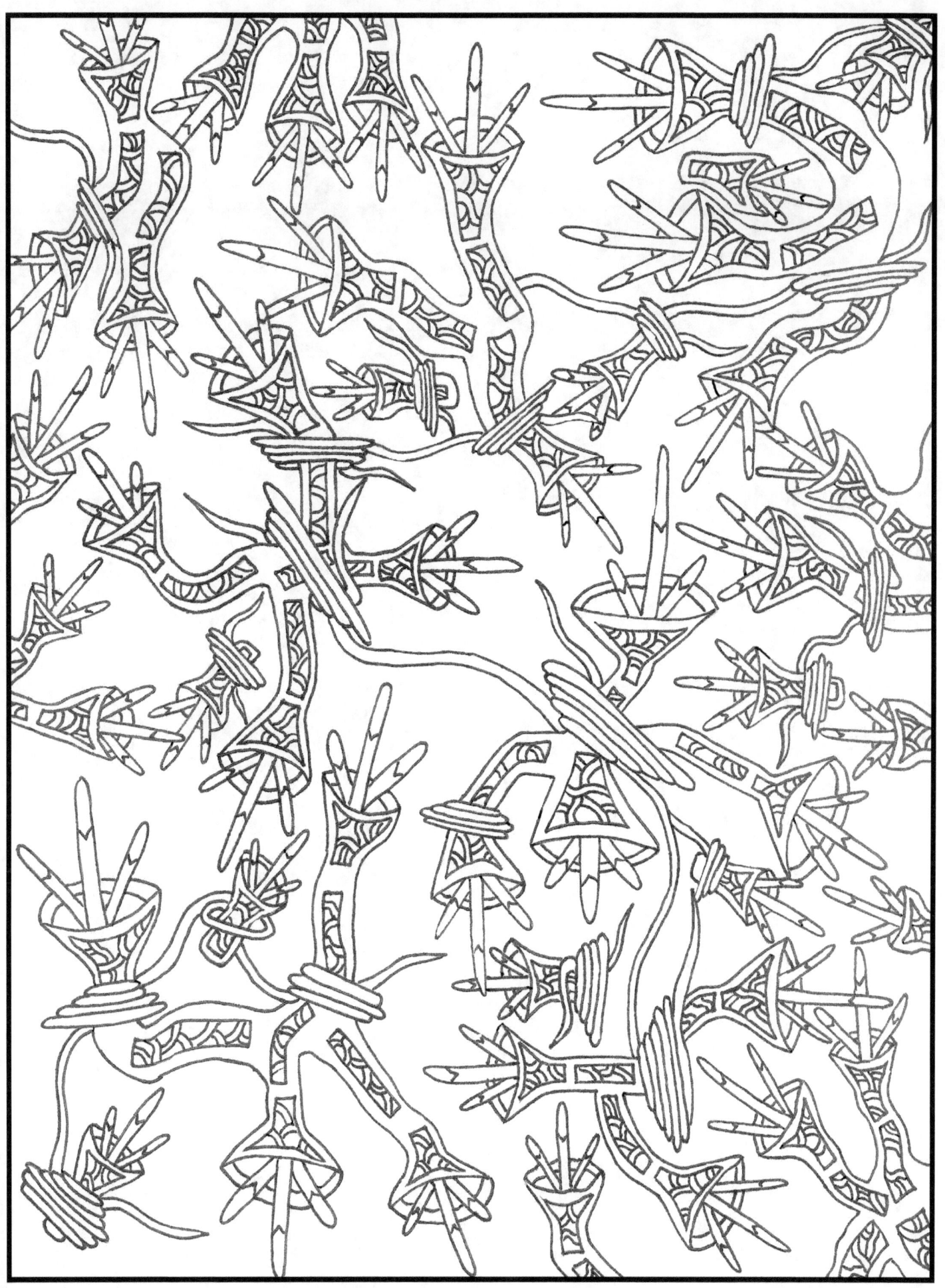

© Damone Heins

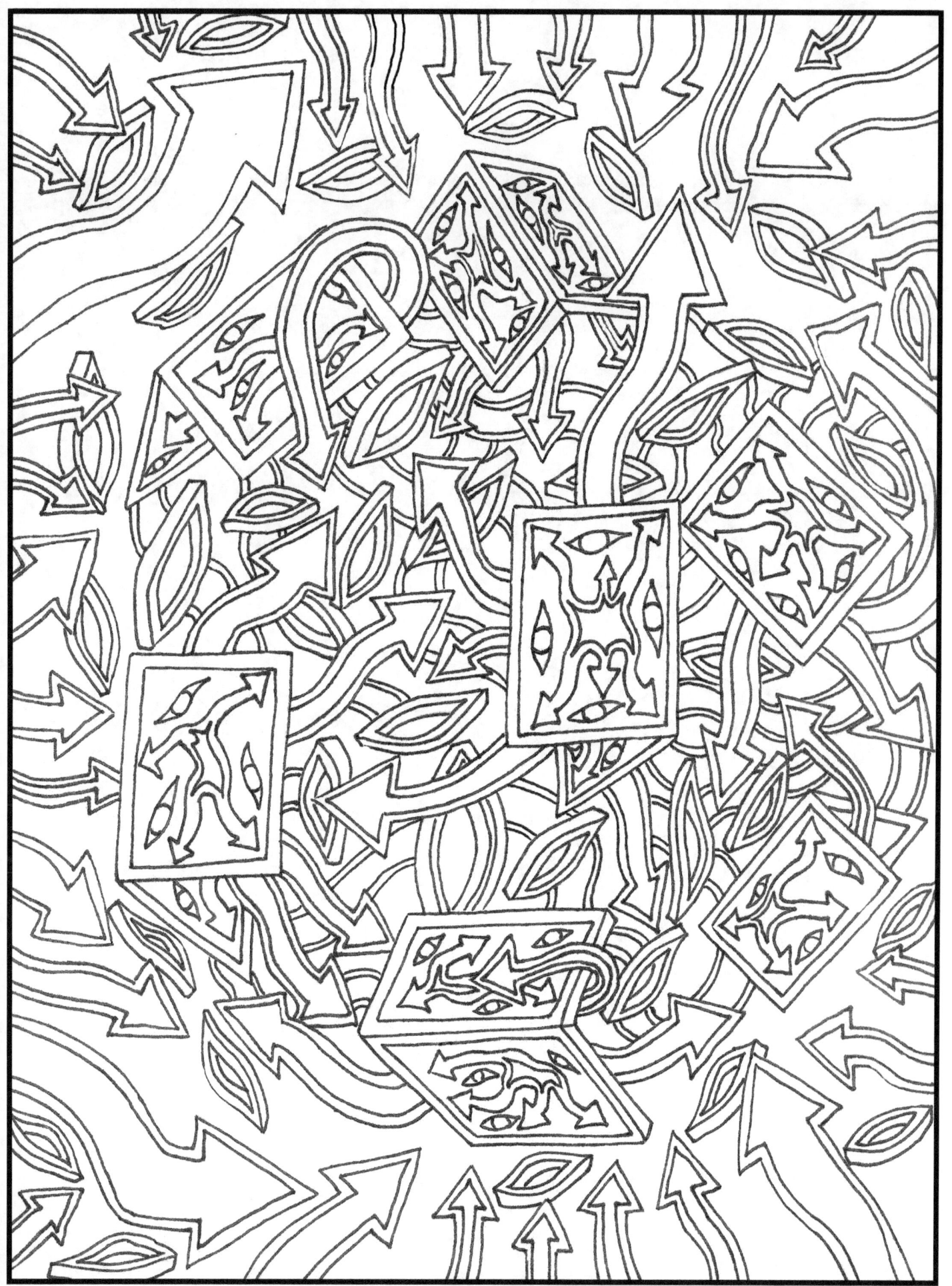

© Damone Heins

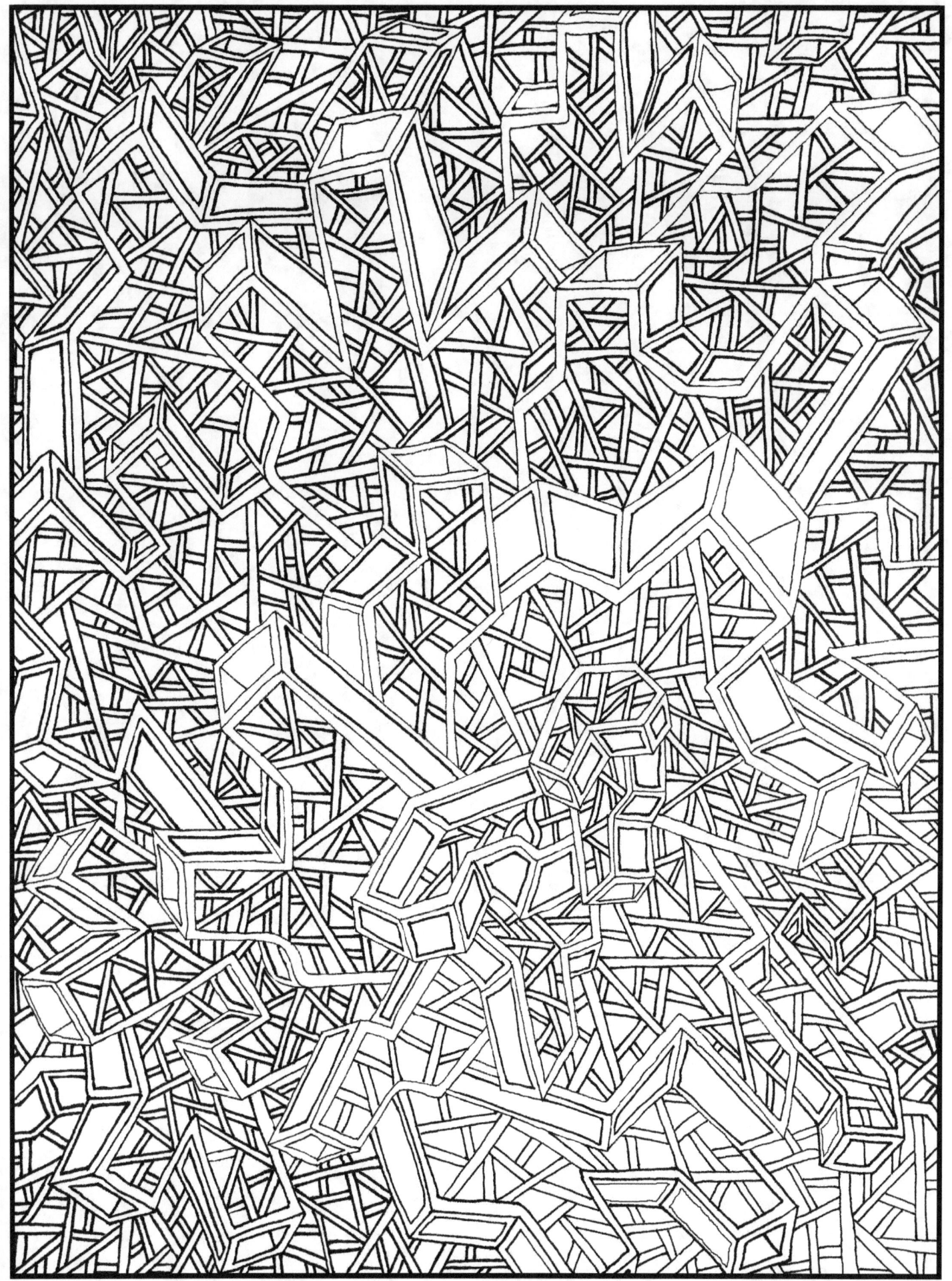

© Damone Heins

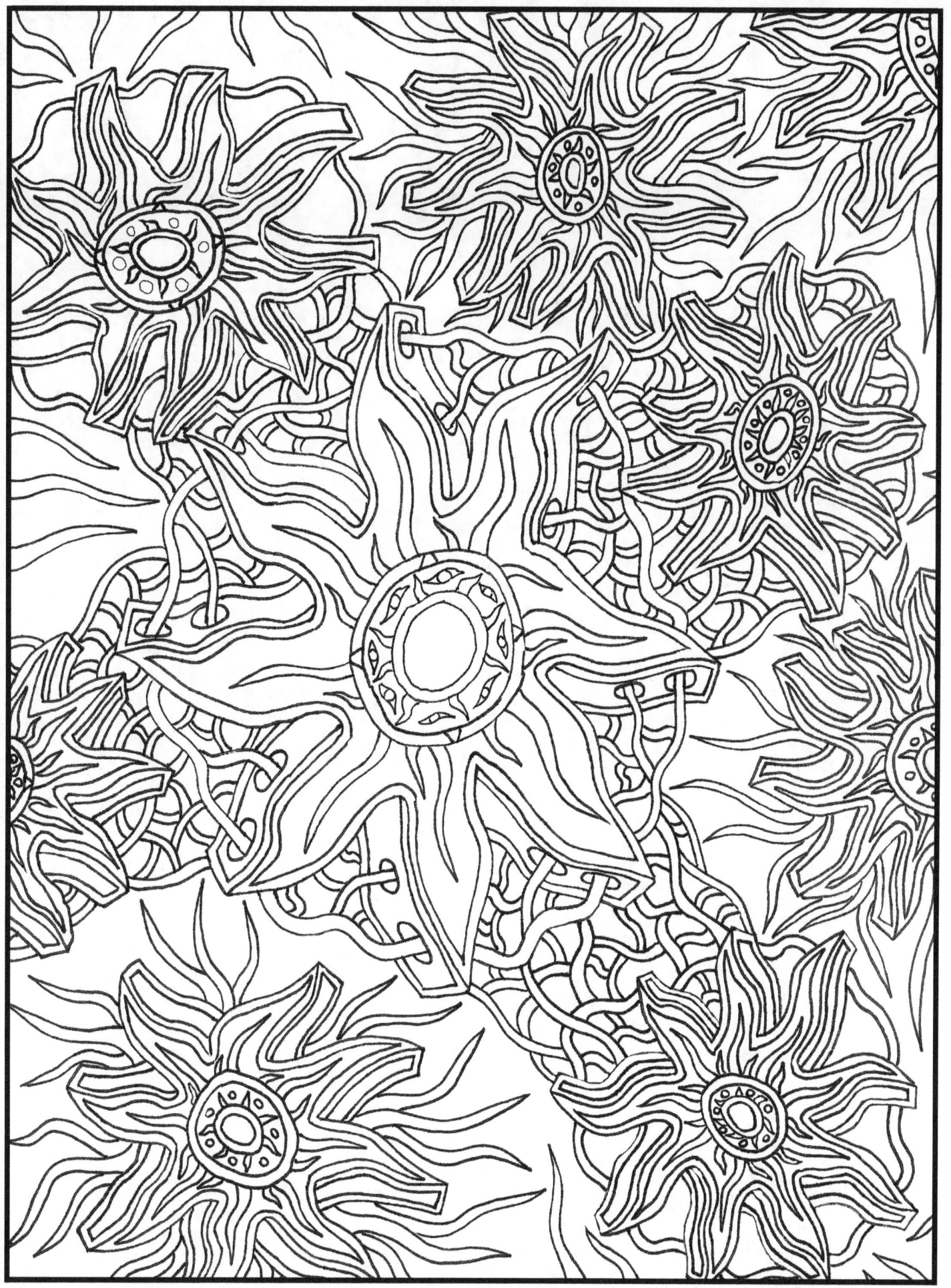

© Damone Heins

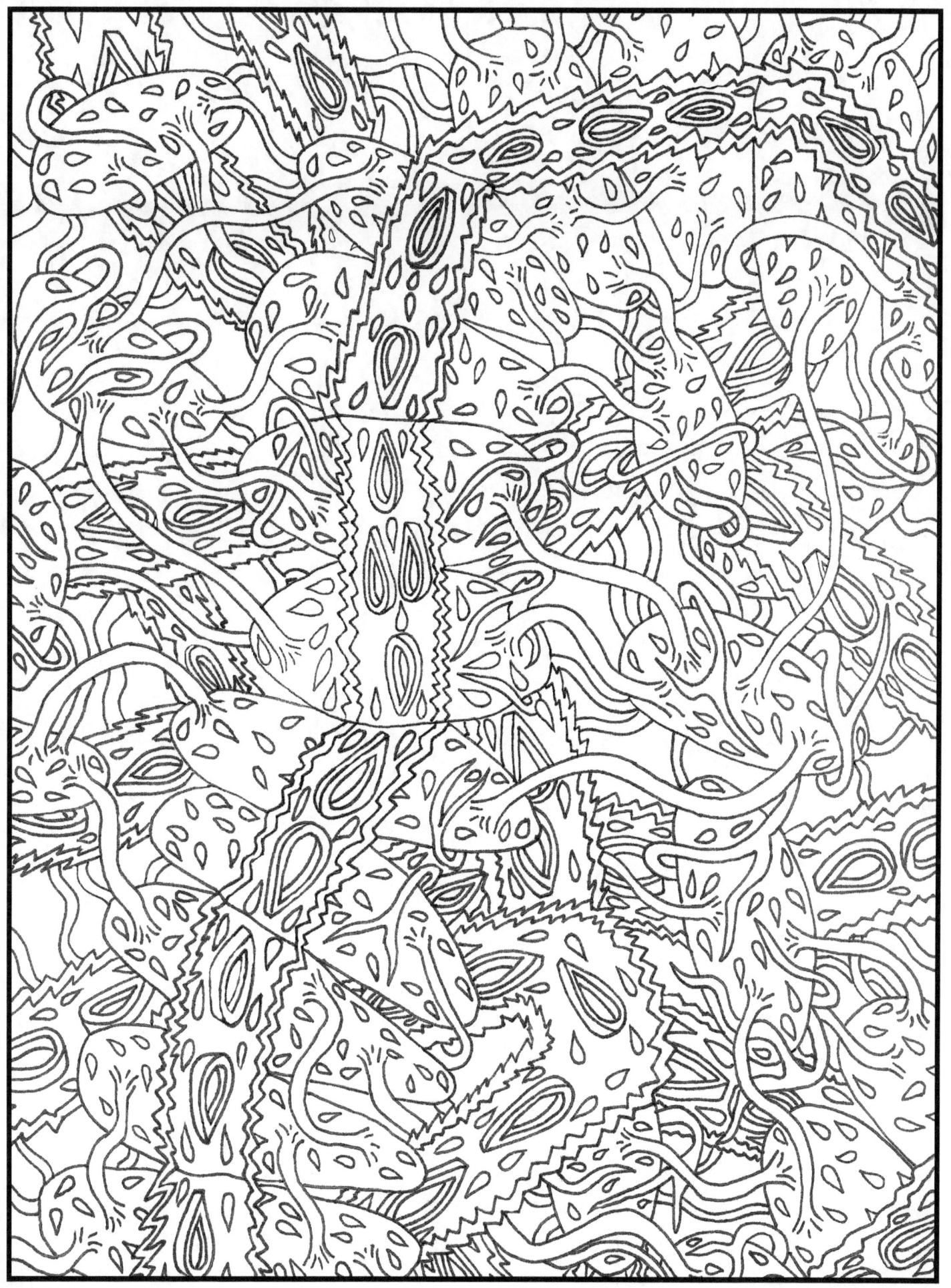

© Damone Heins

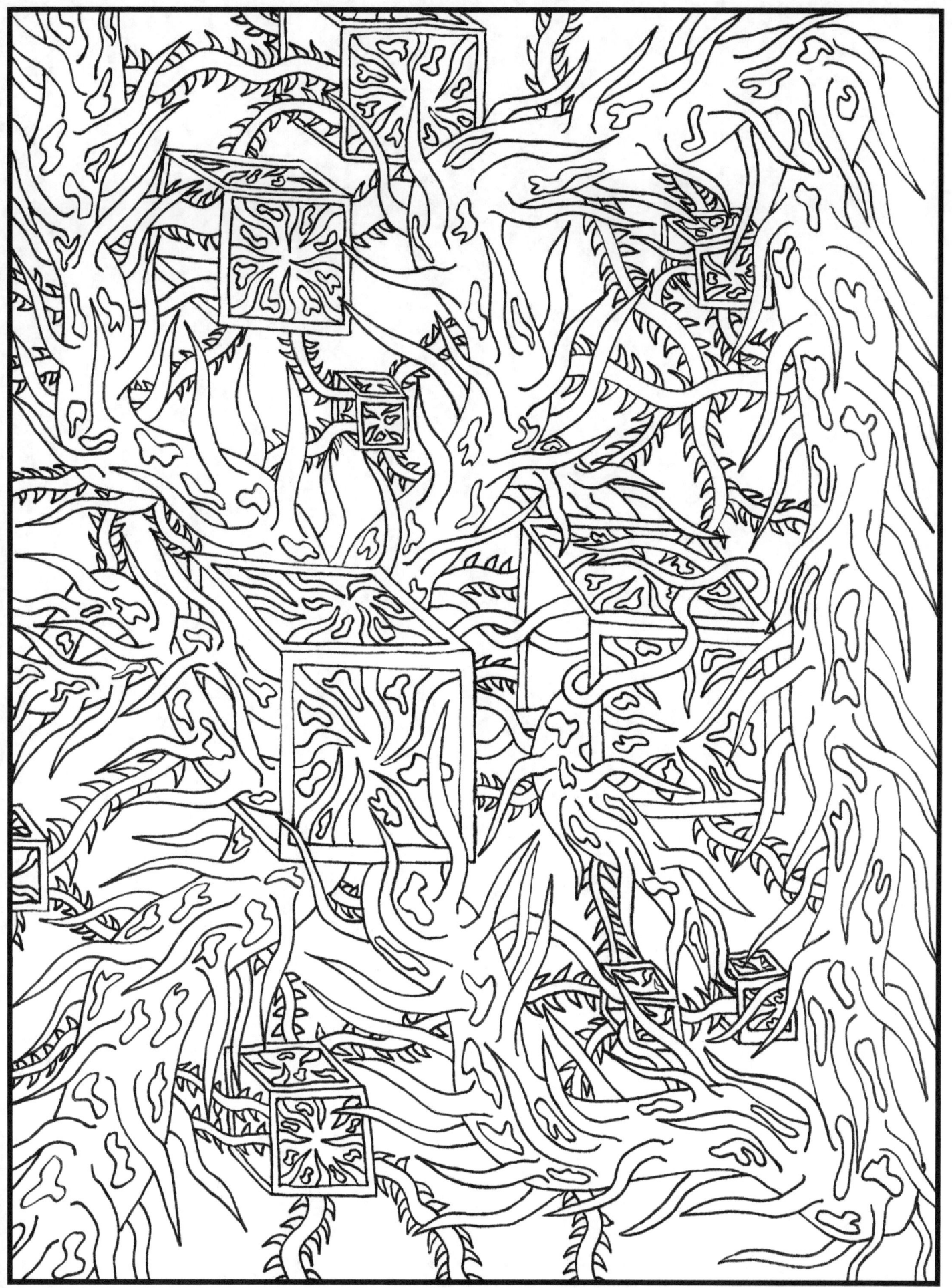

© Damone Heins

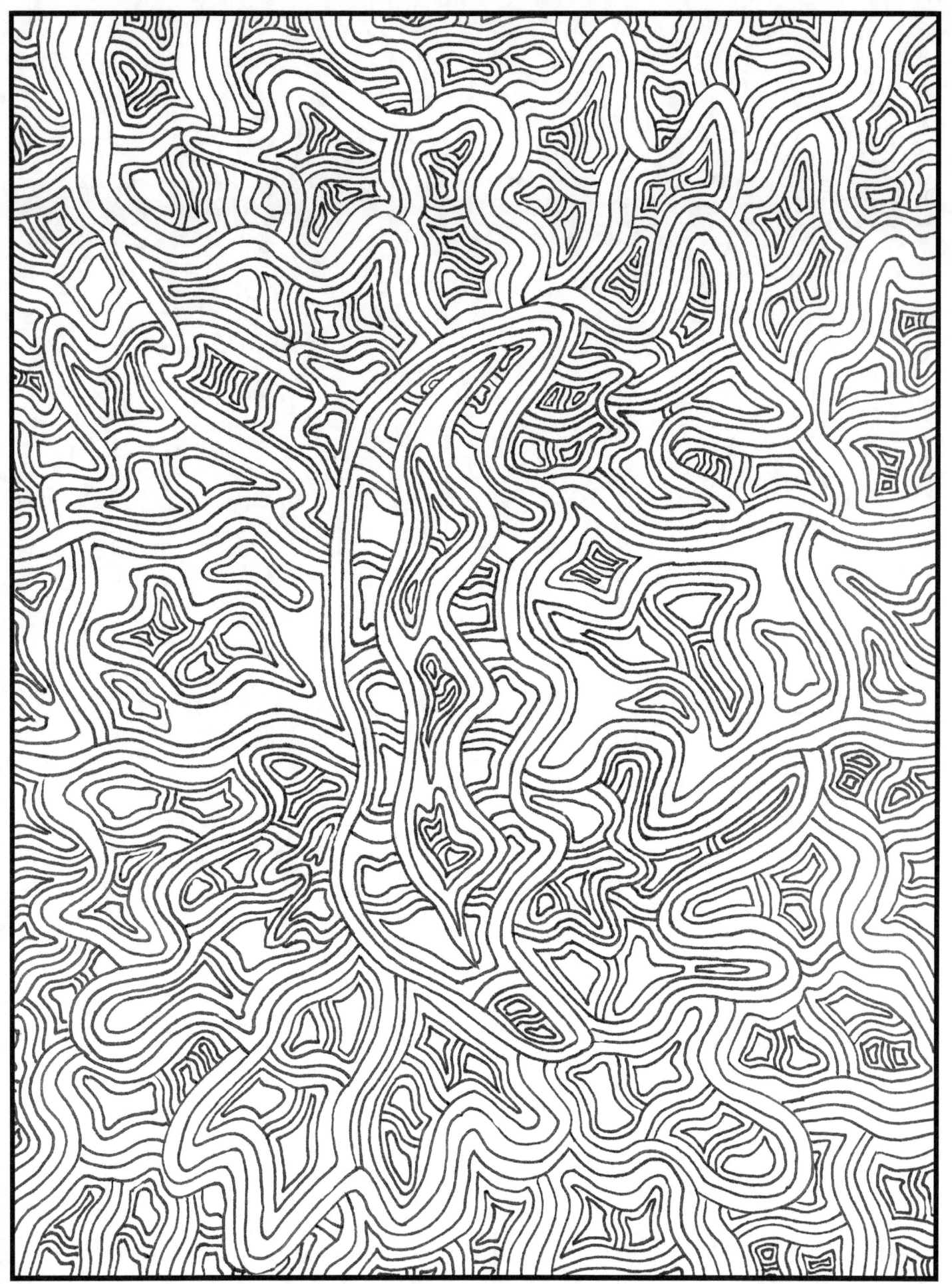

© Damone Heins

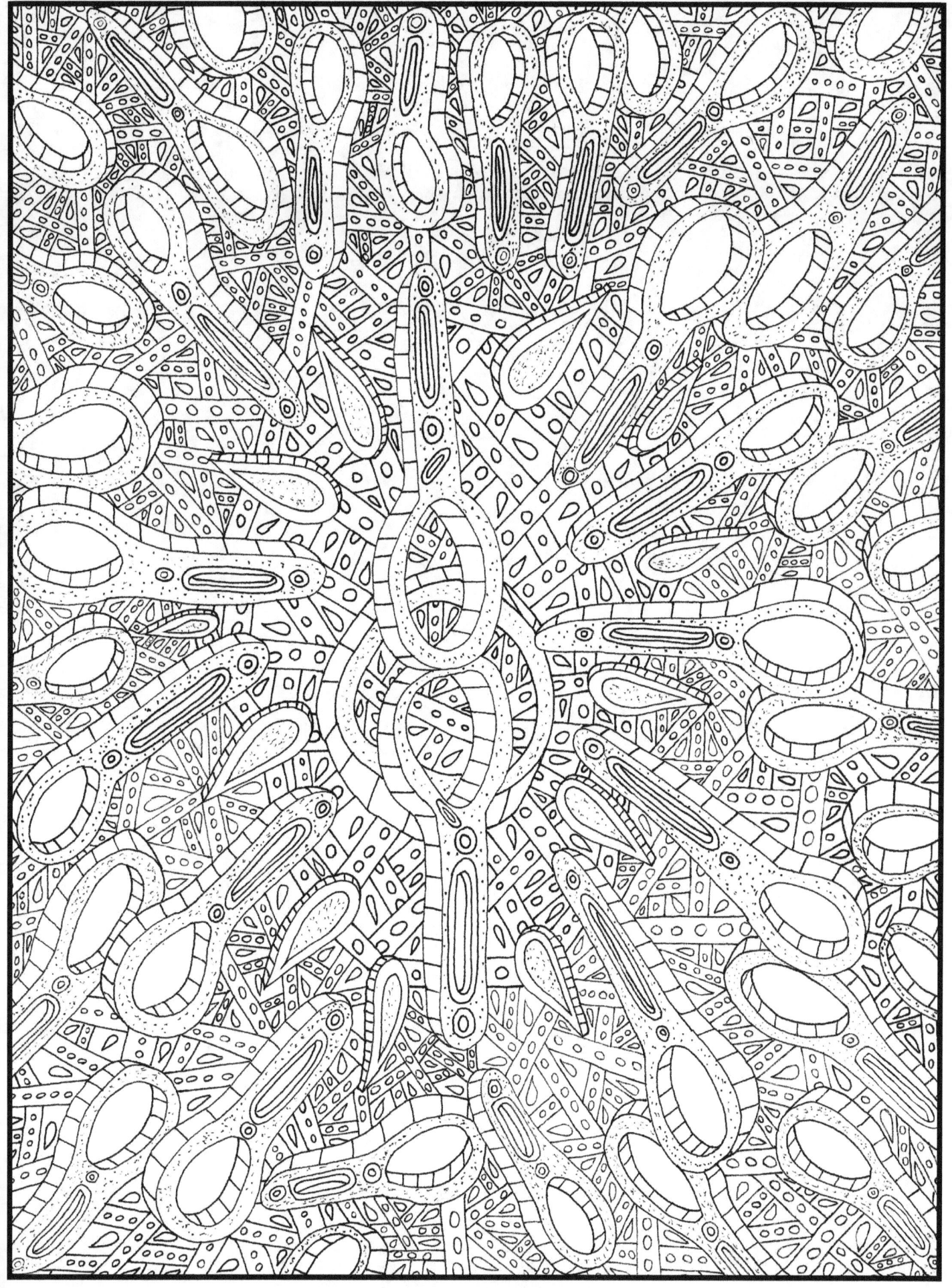

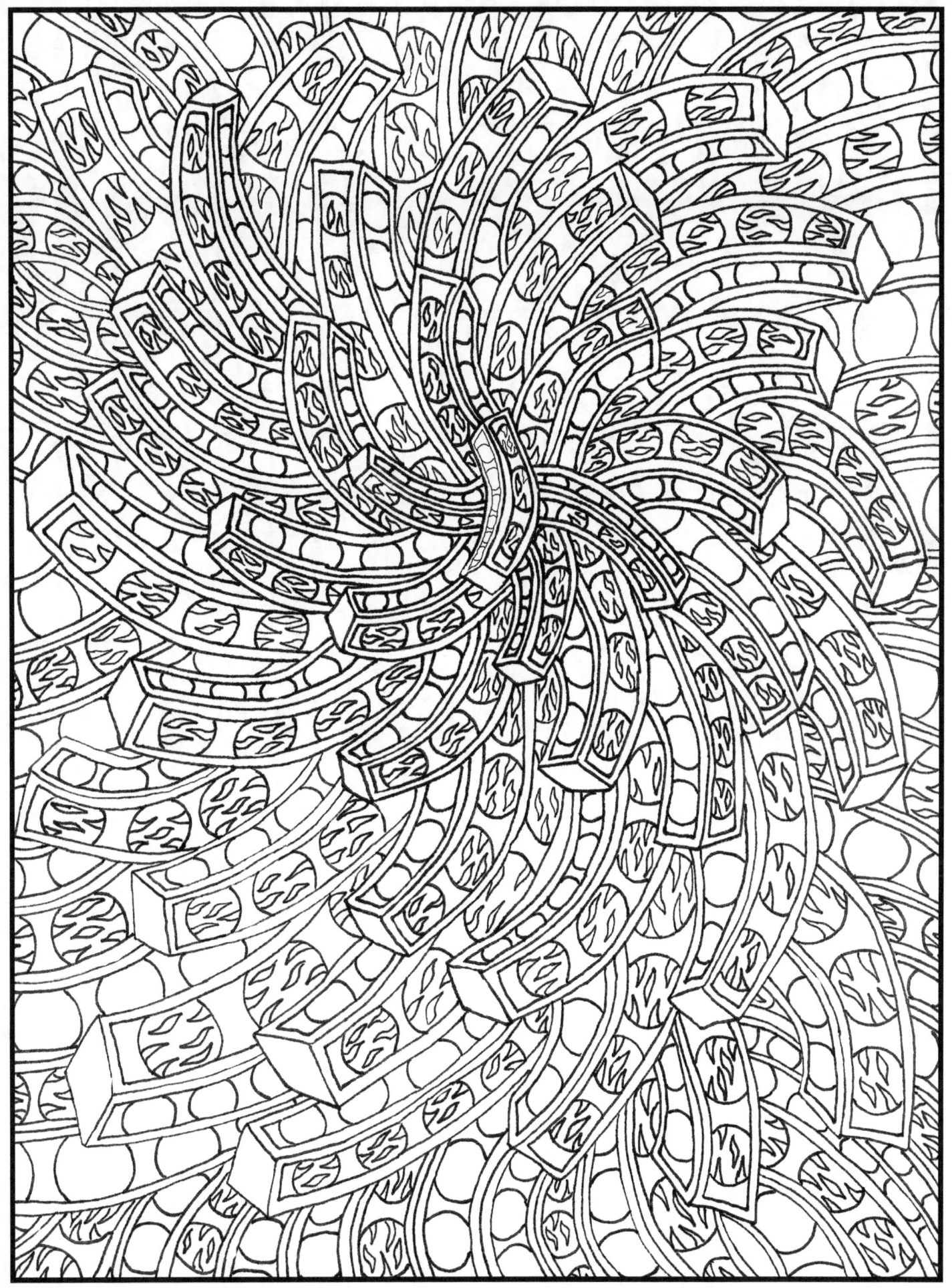

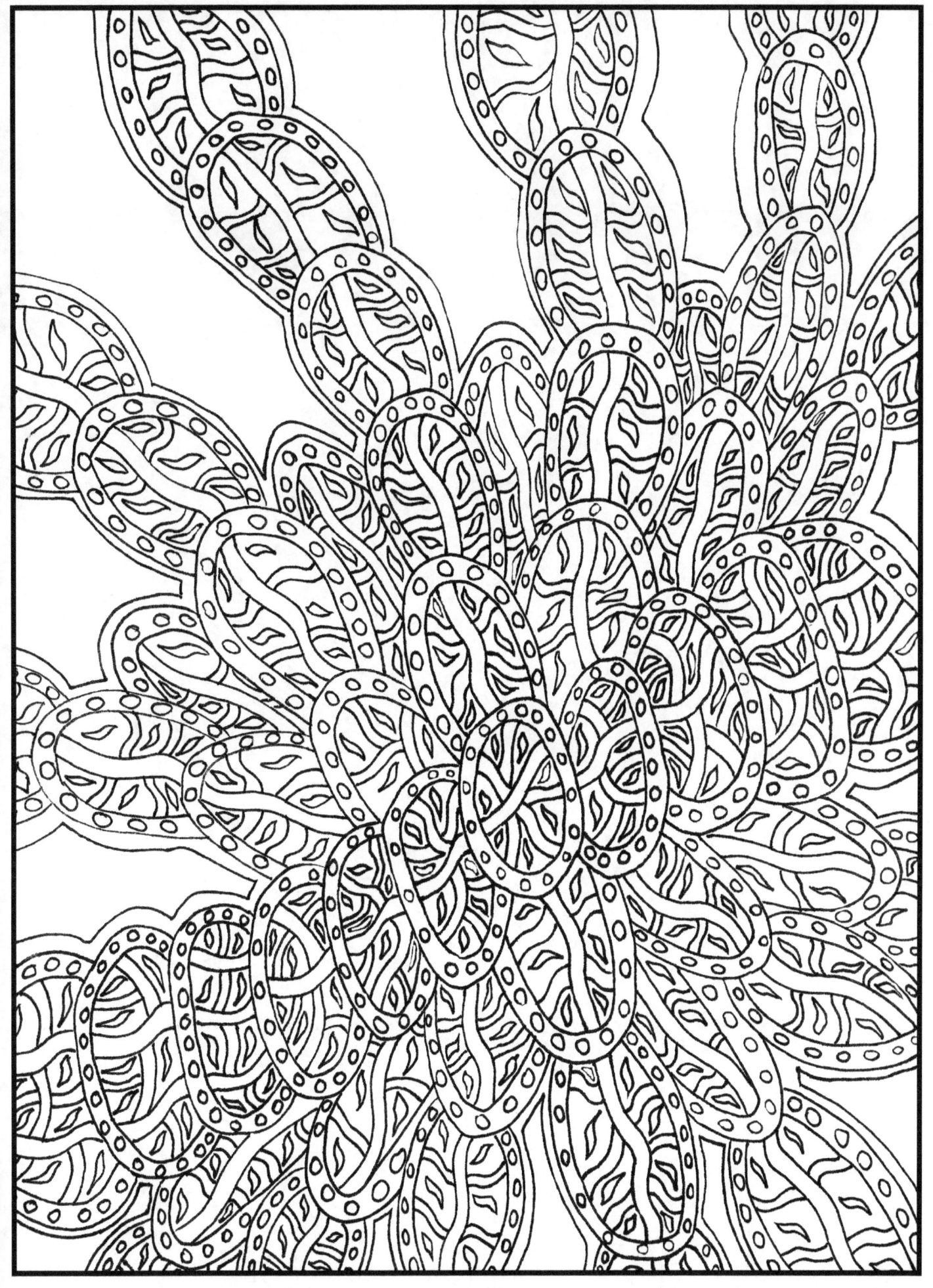

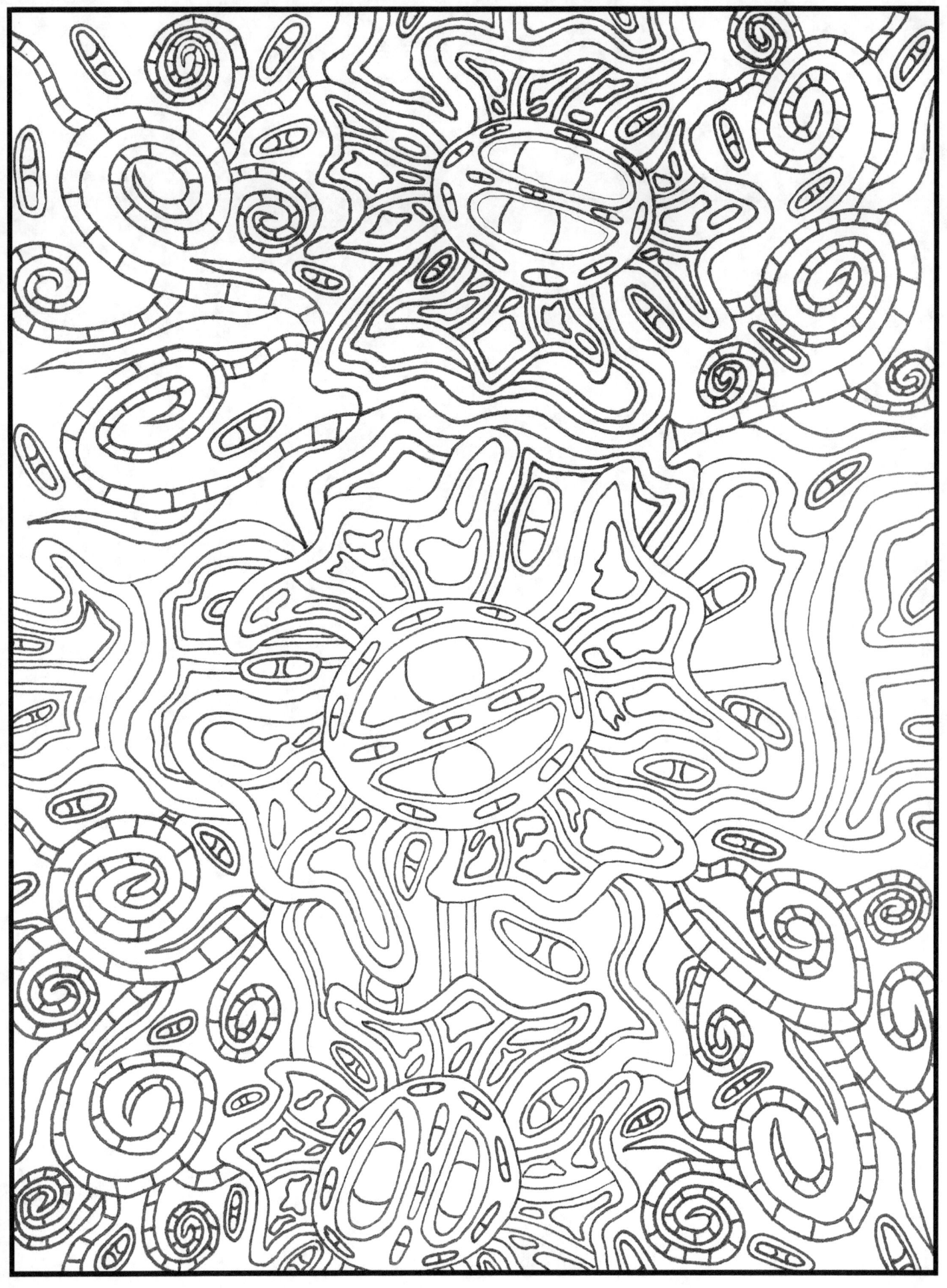

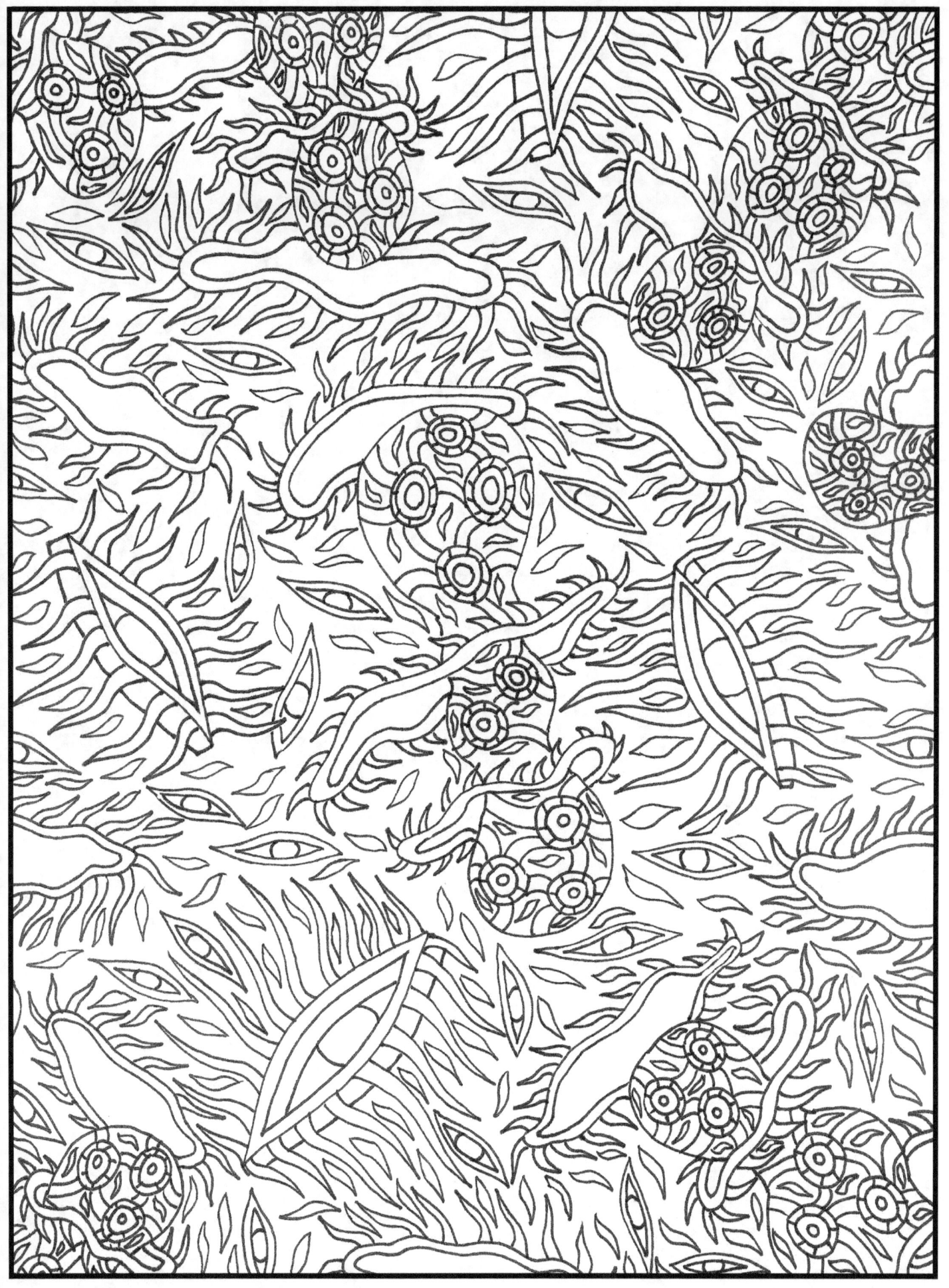

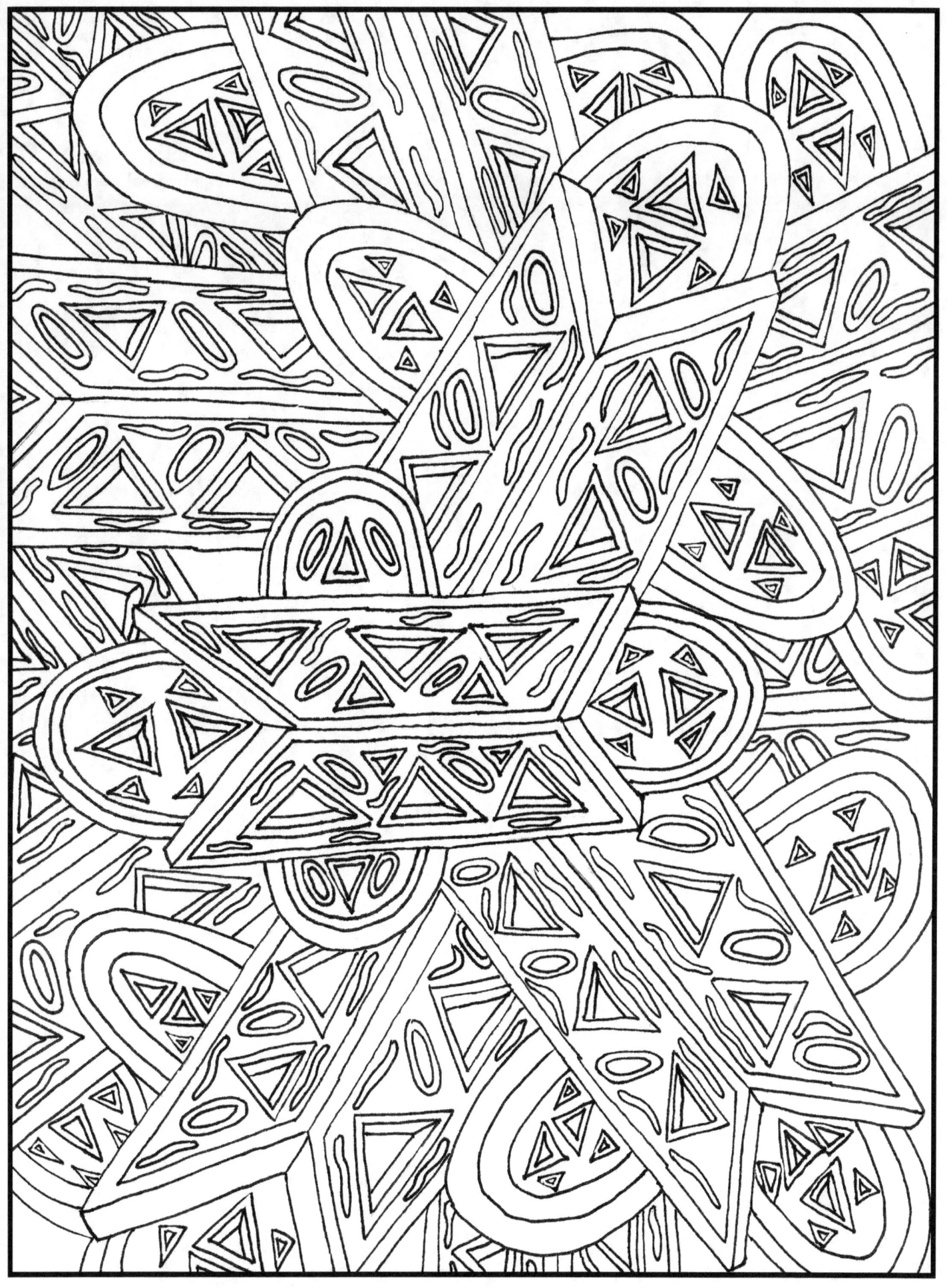

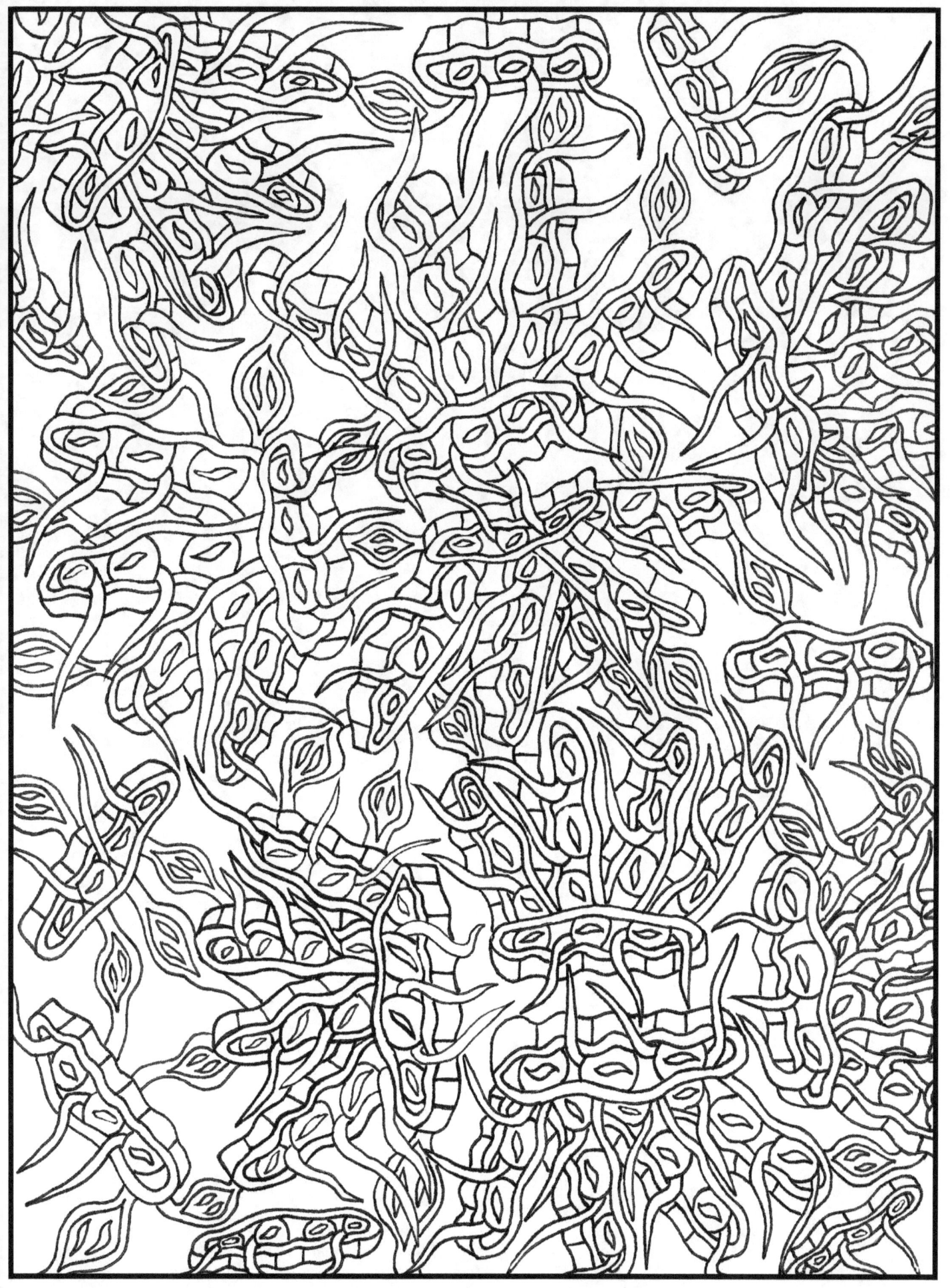

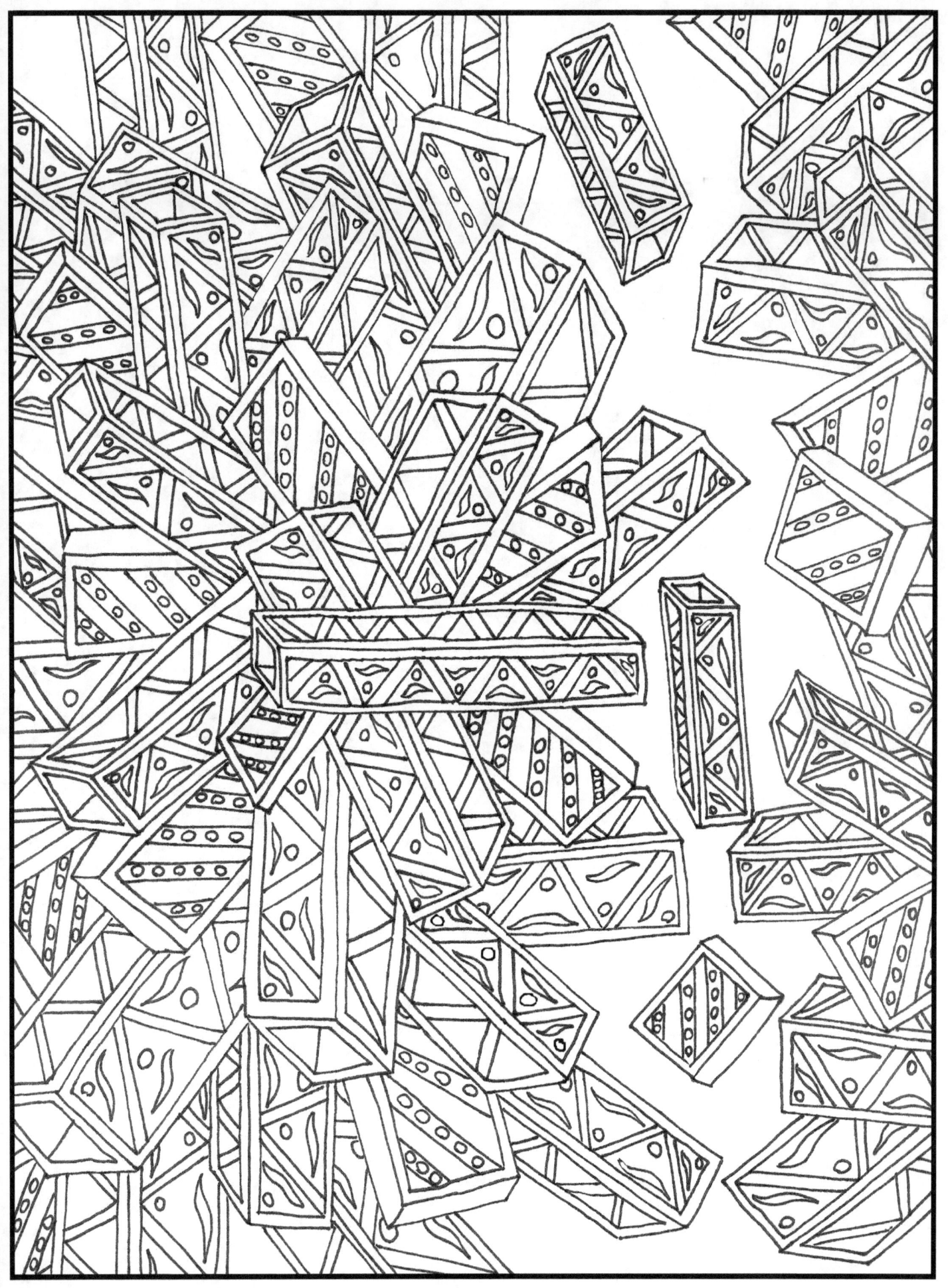

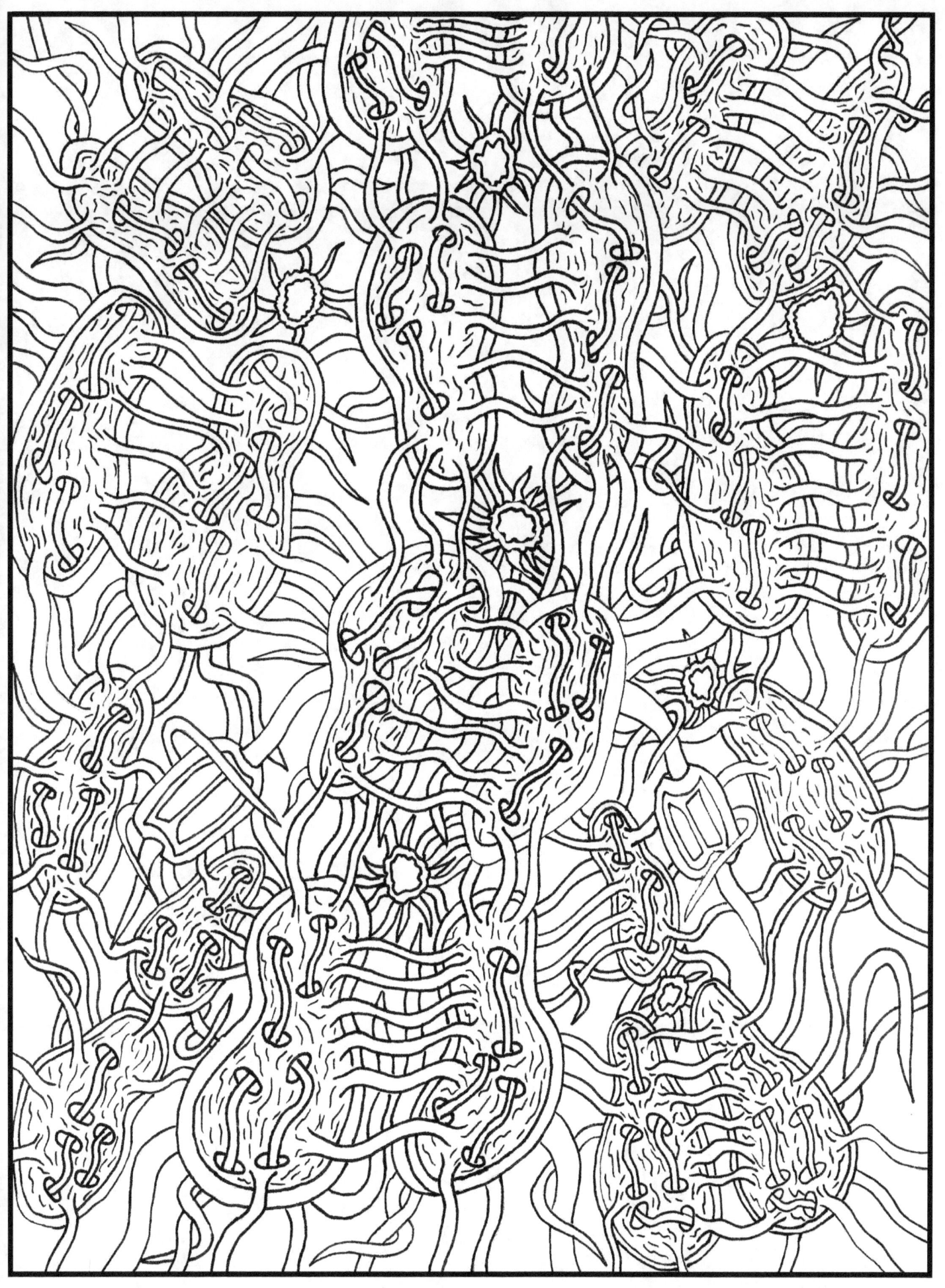

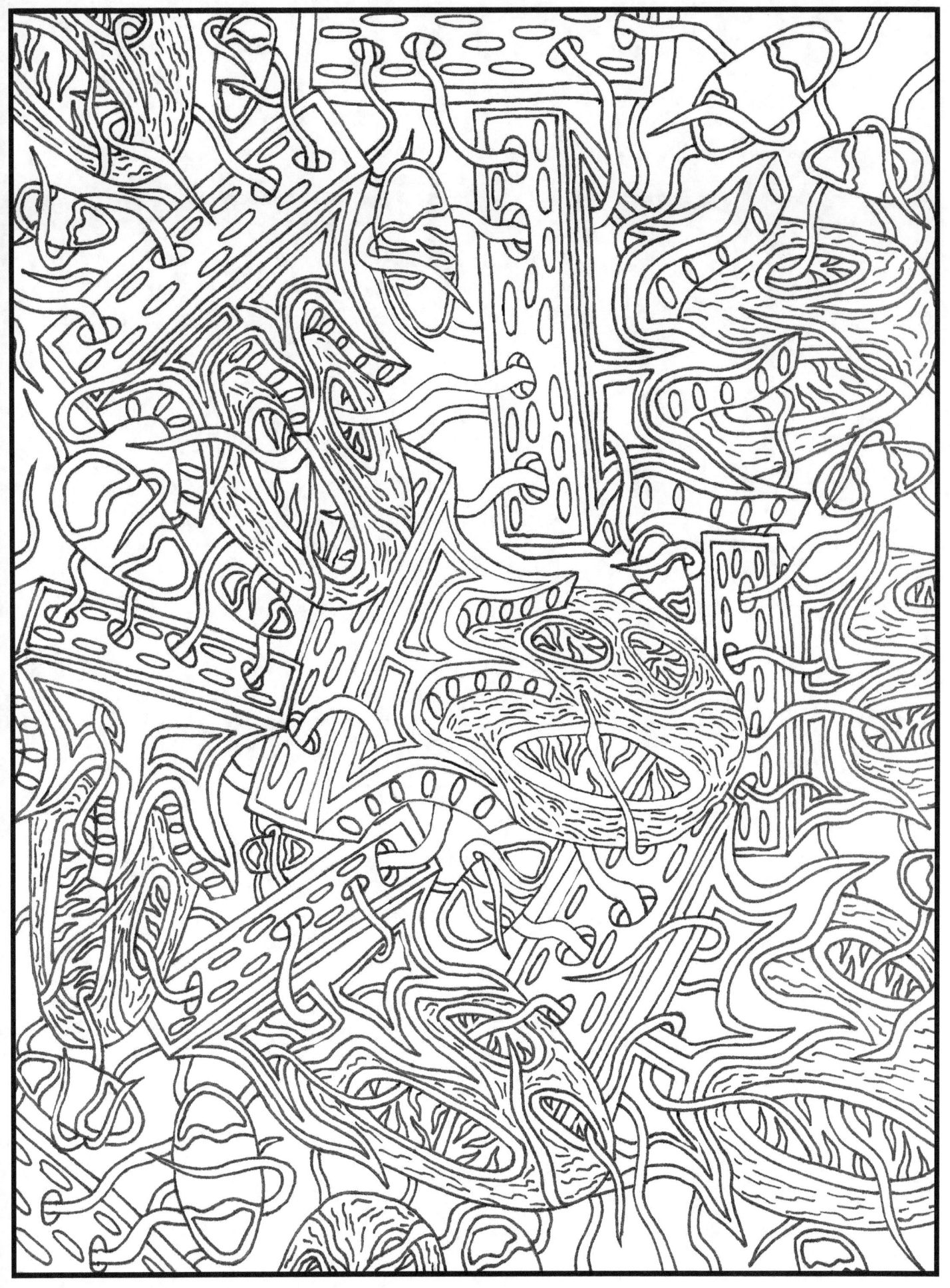

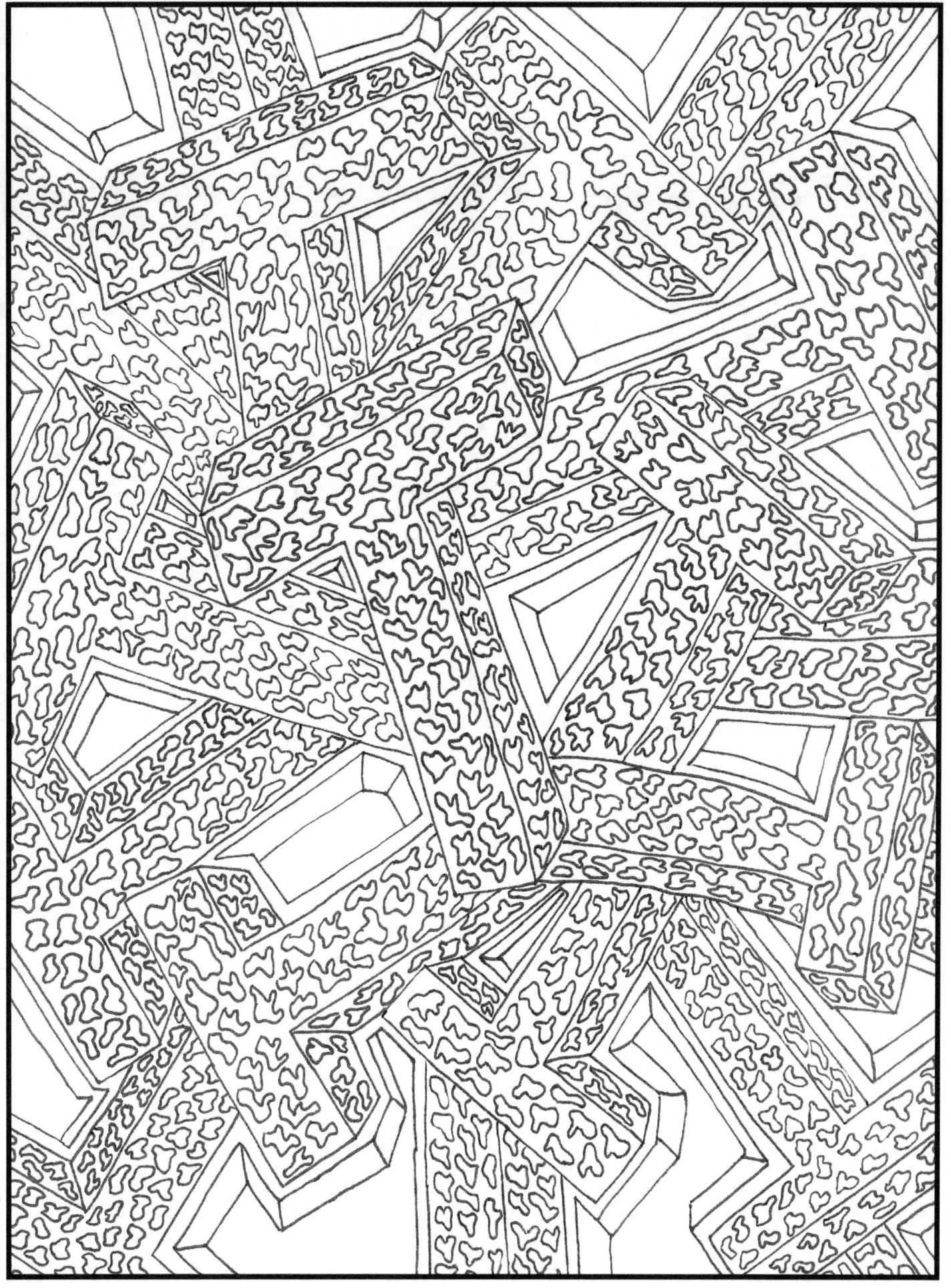

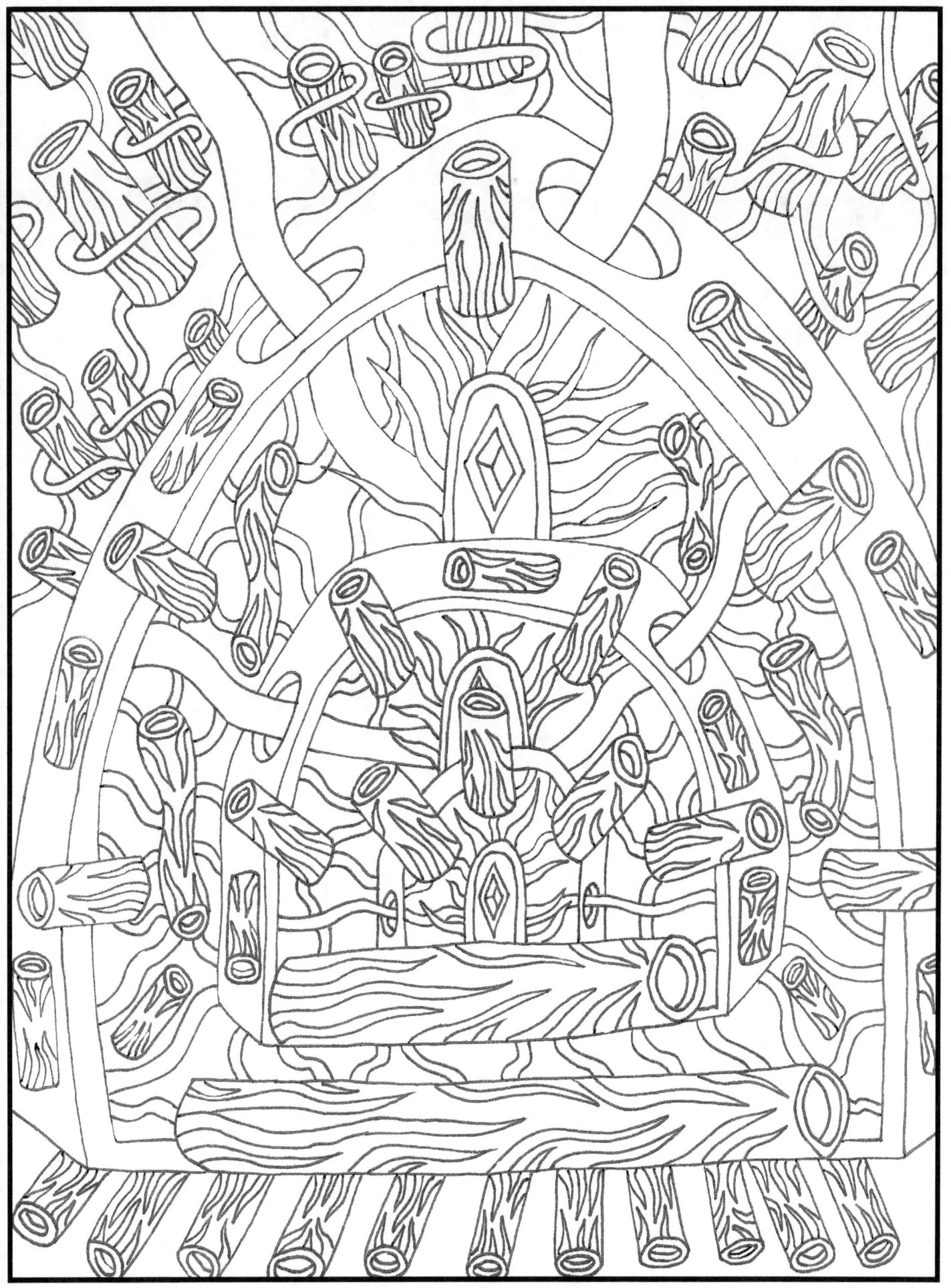

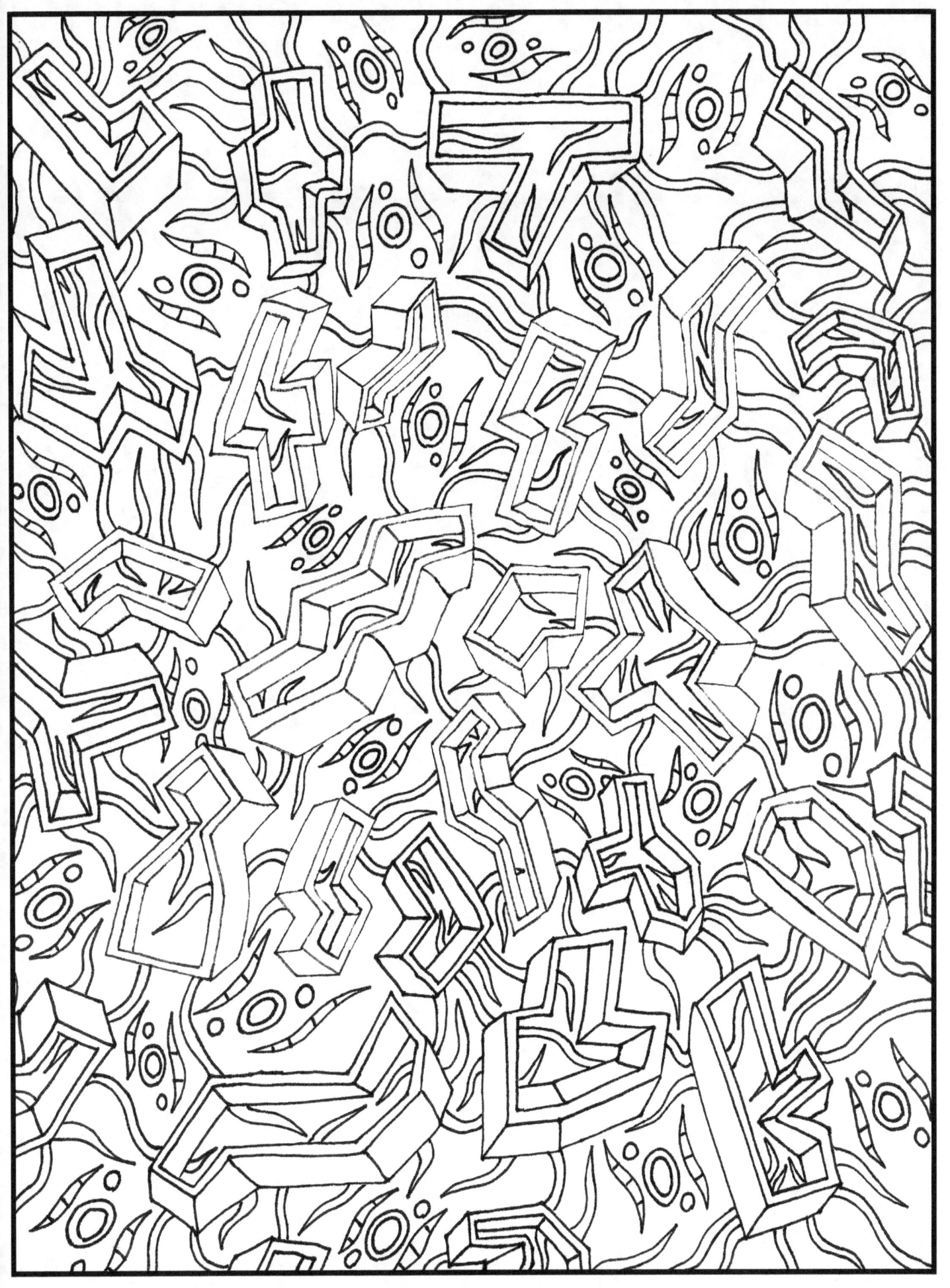

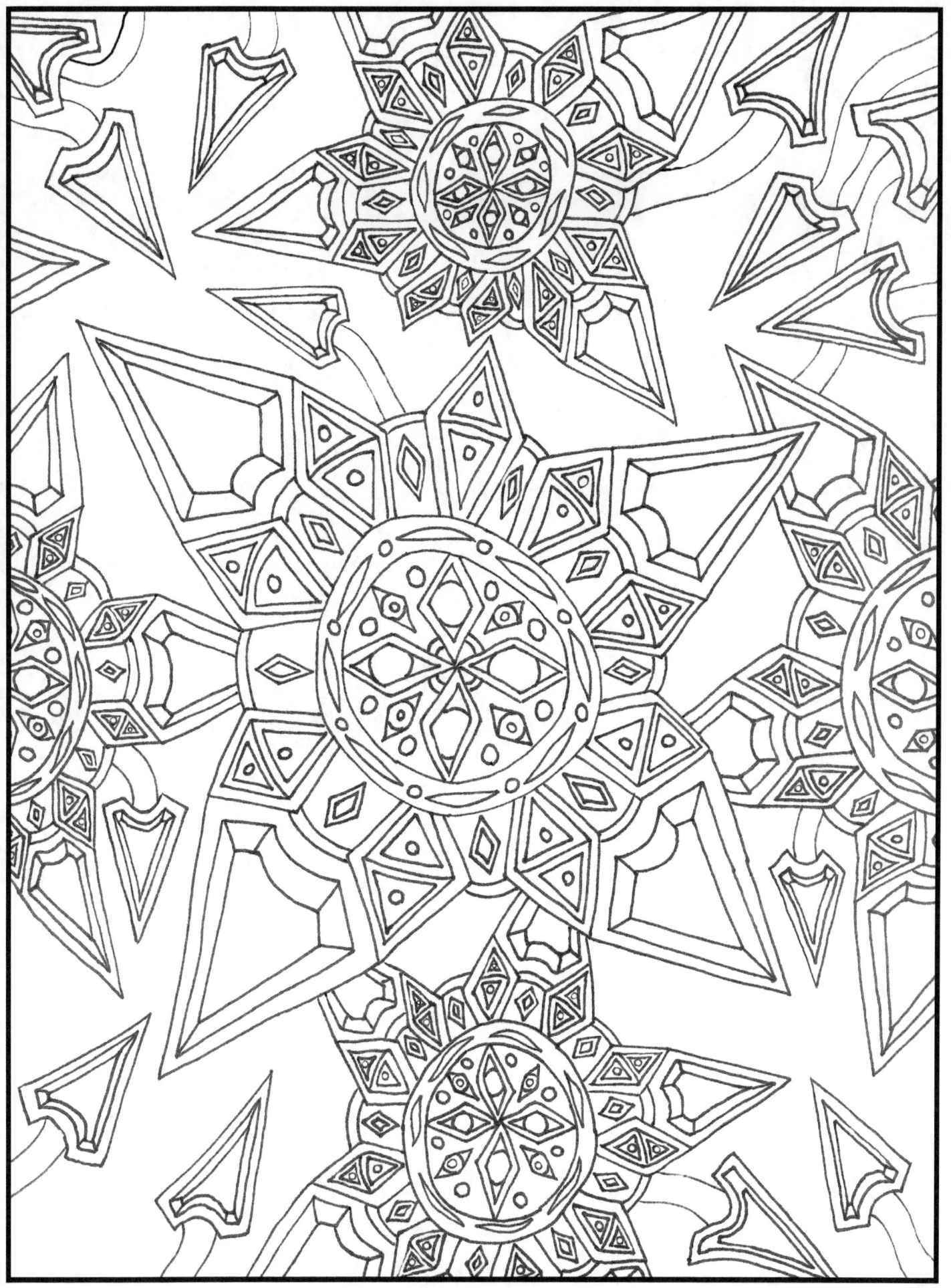

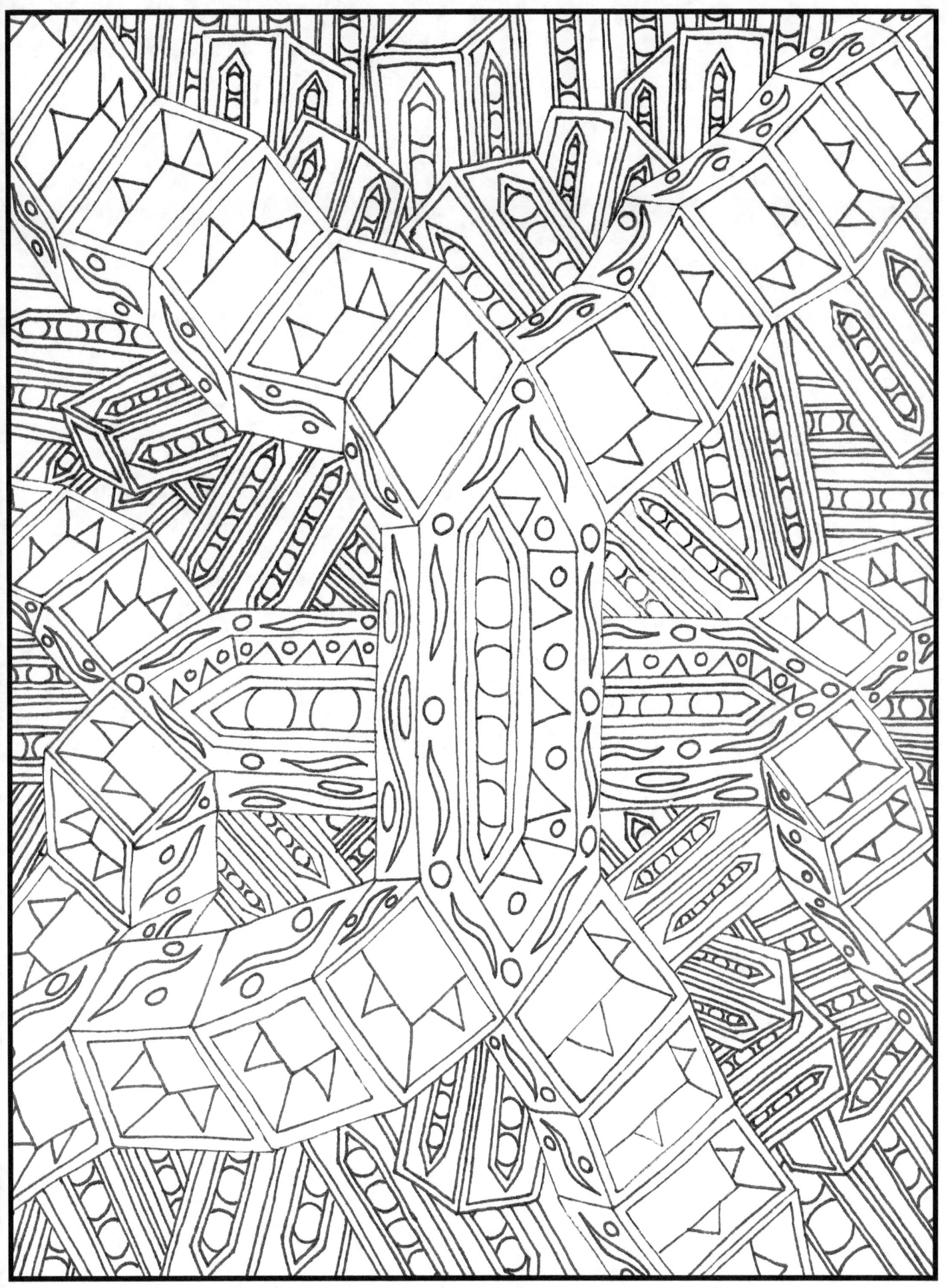

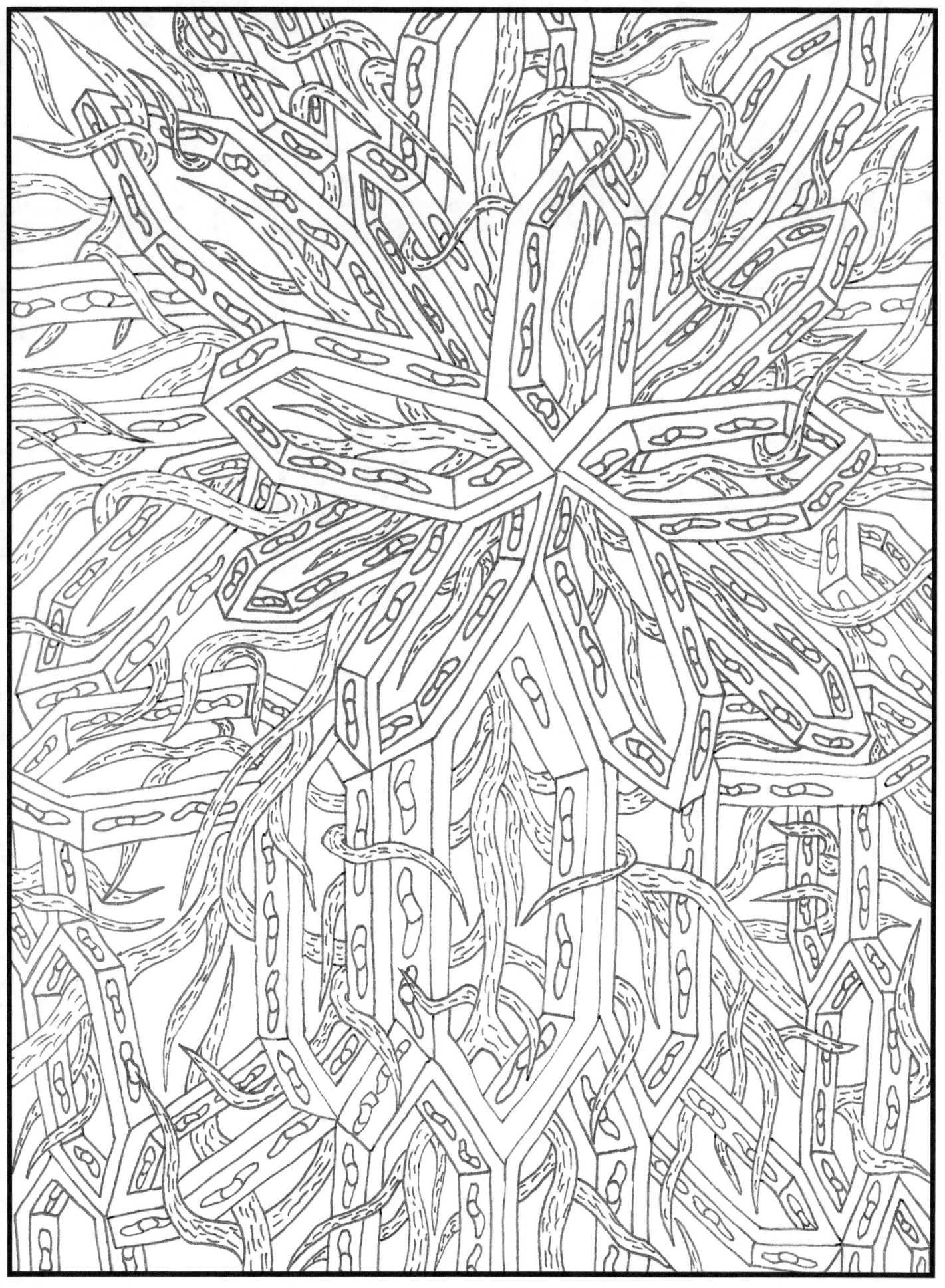

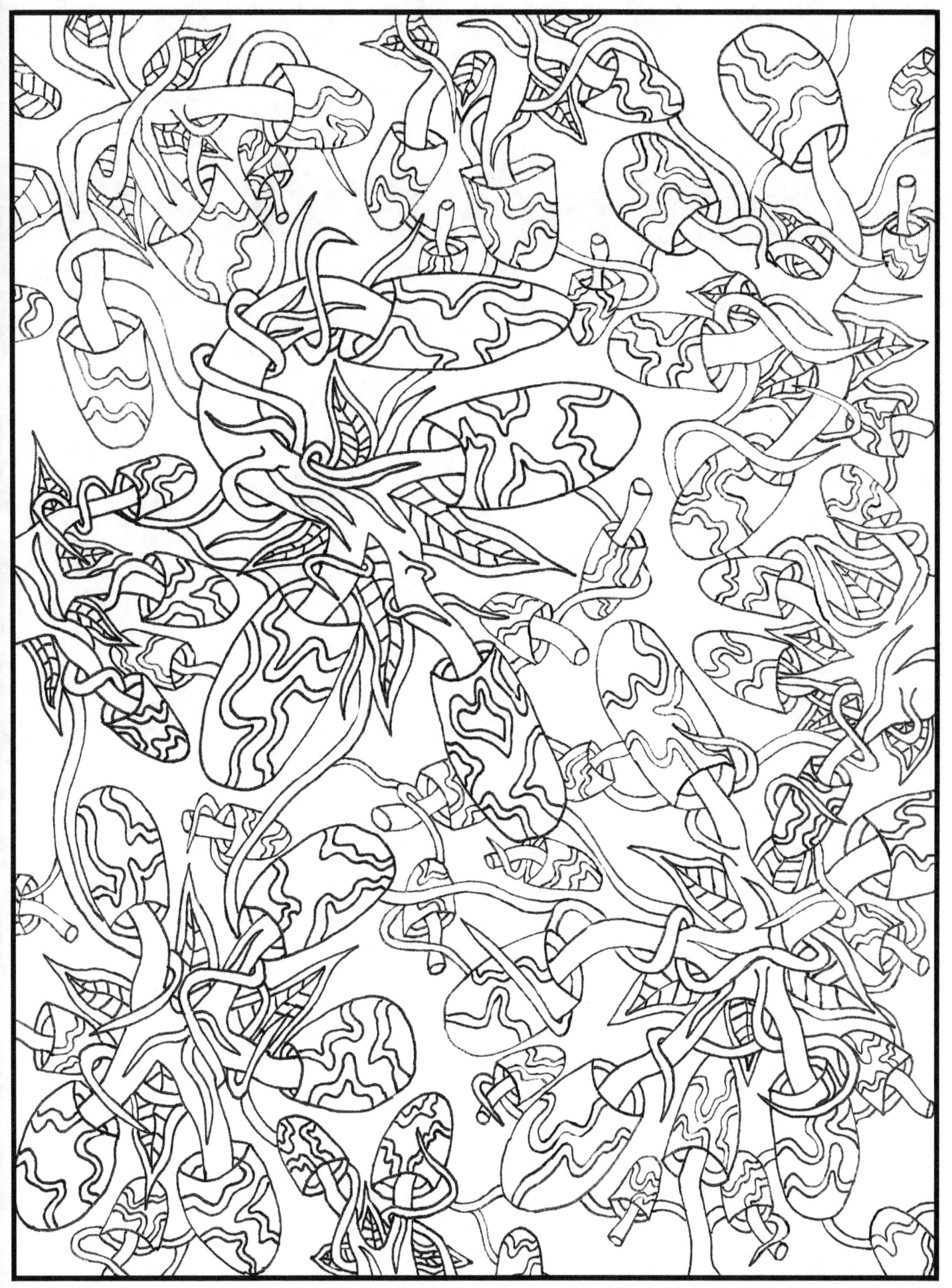

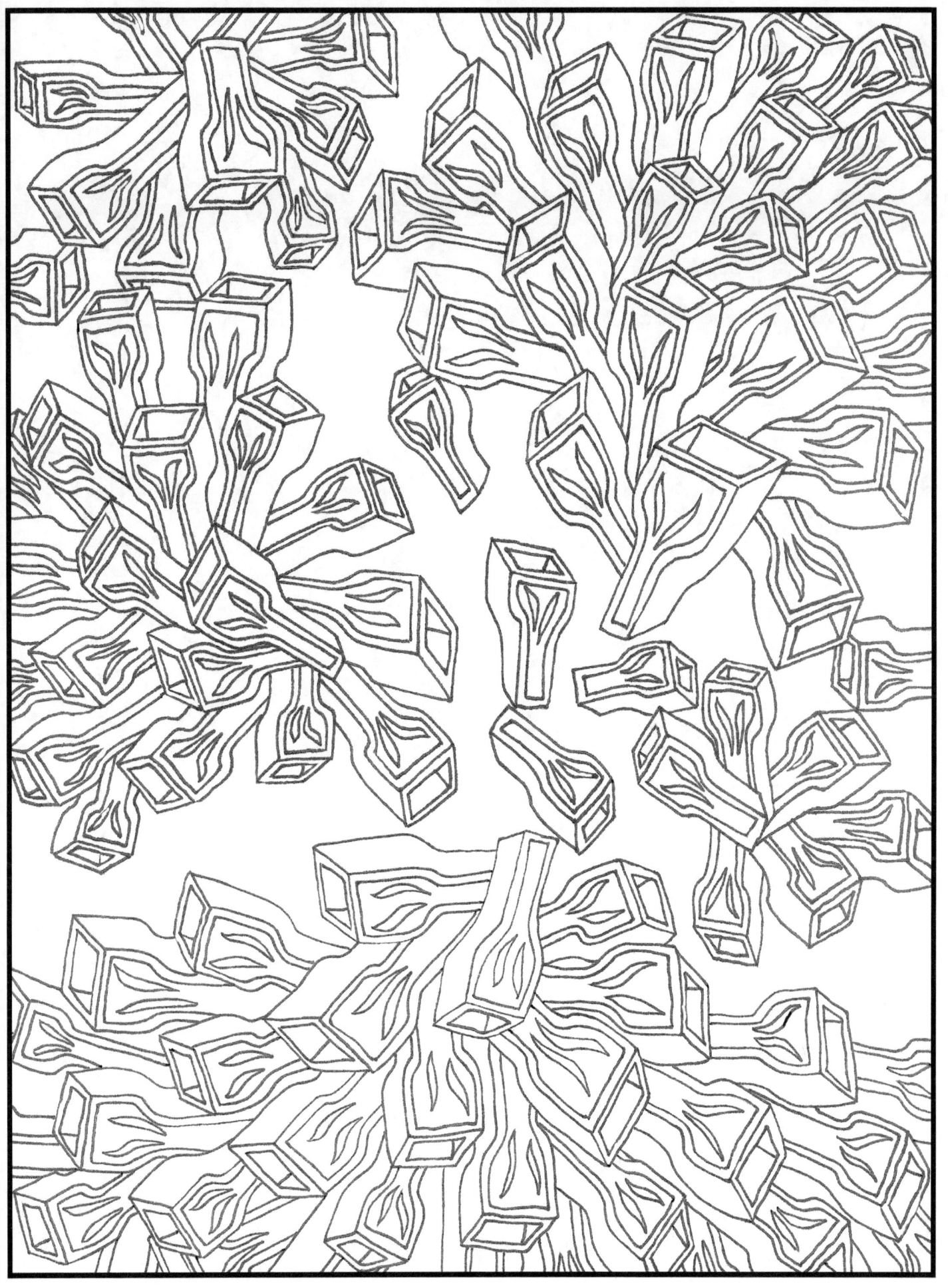

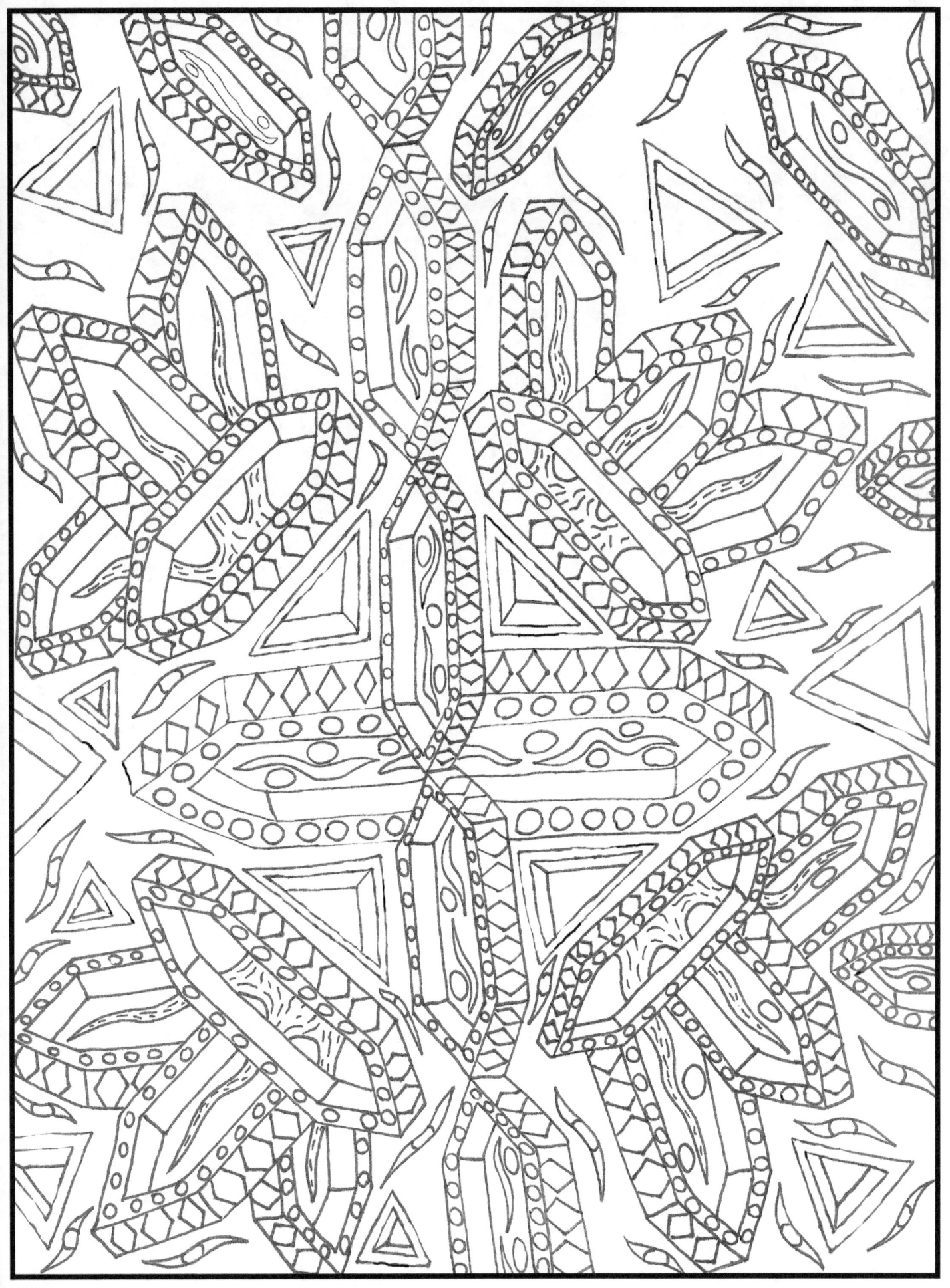

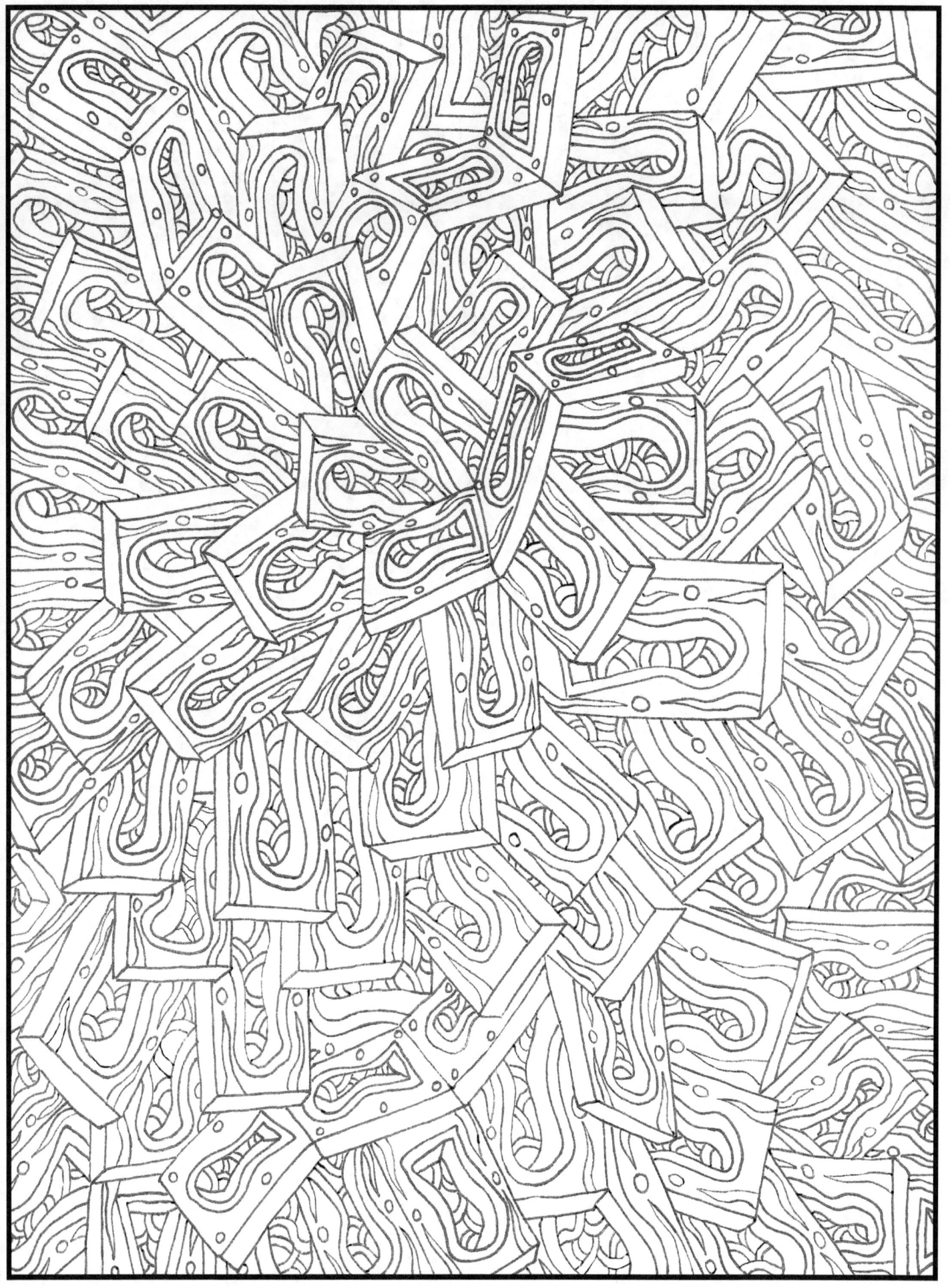

For more books
email me at damonehe@yahoo.com
or mail me at PO. box
2433 Newport Oregon
97365
or you can visit damonesart.com

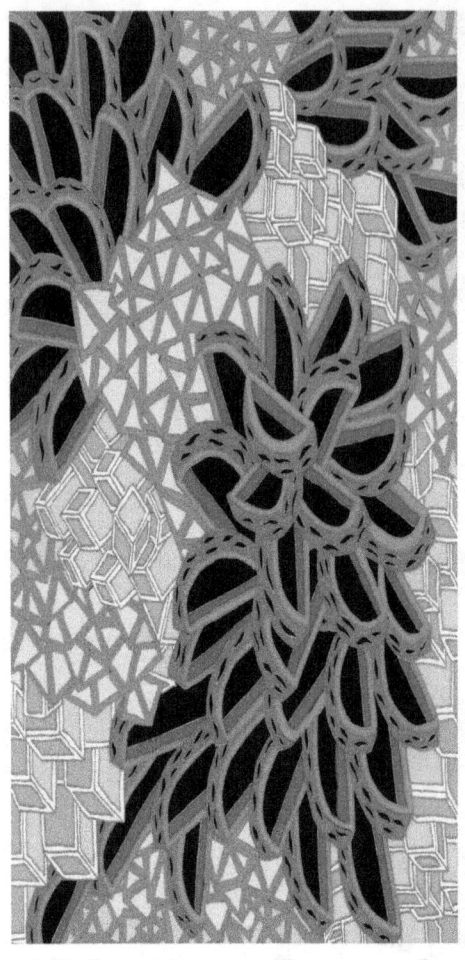
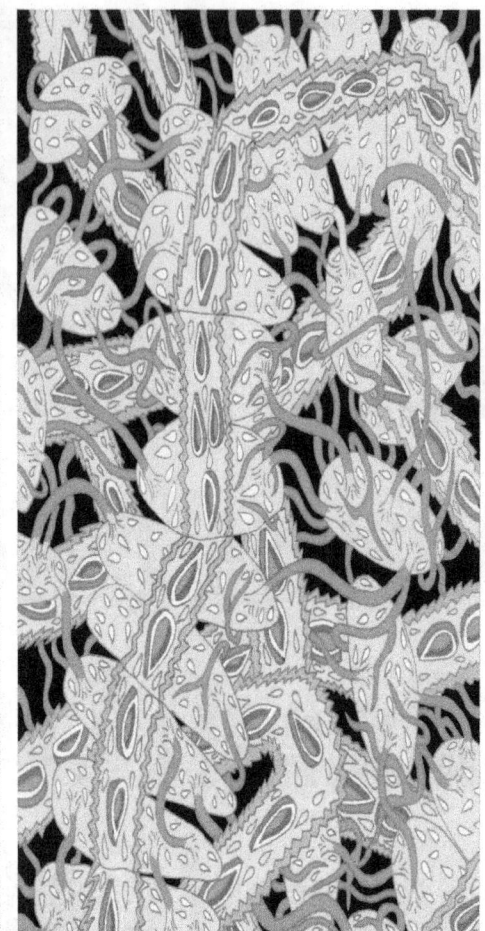
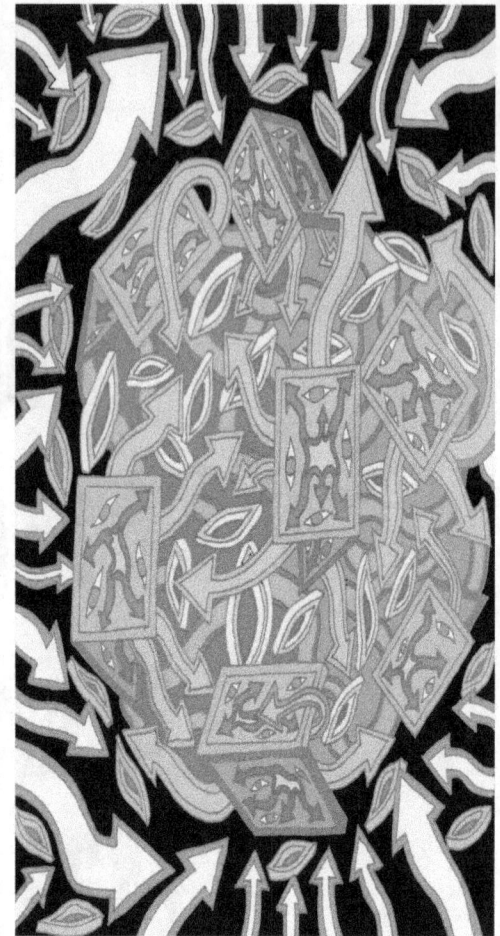

All Art done by Damone Heins

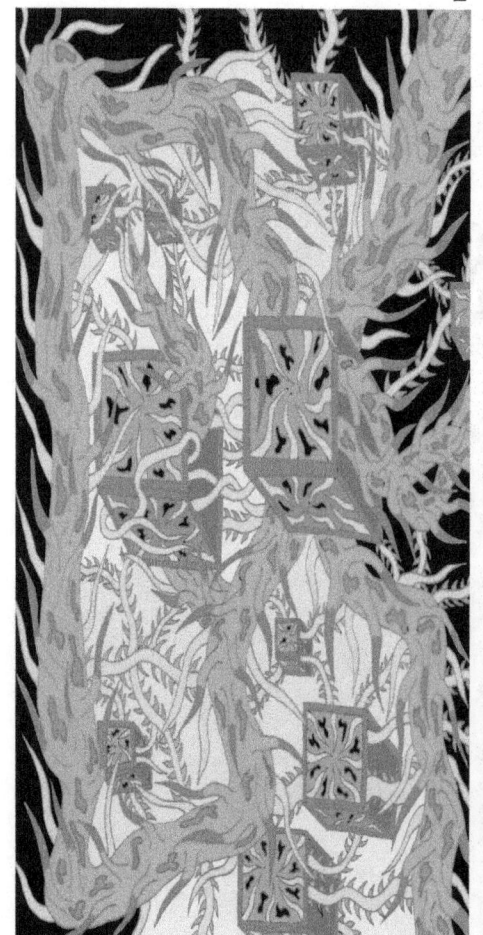
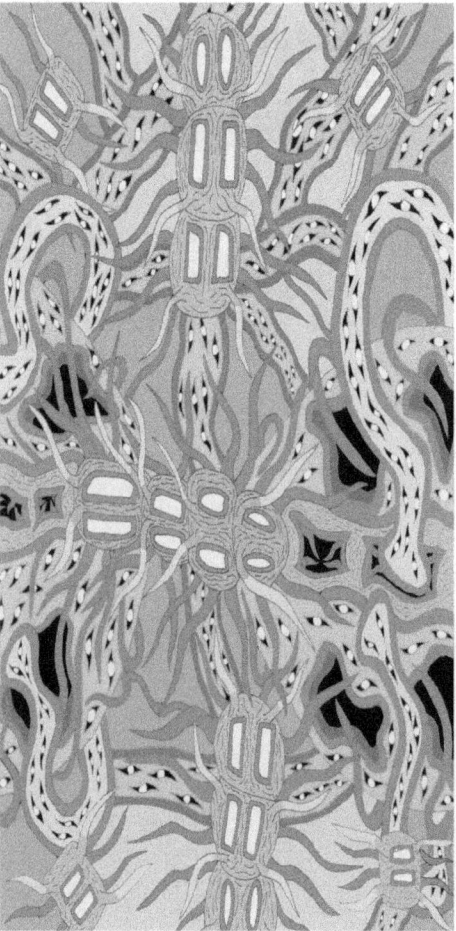
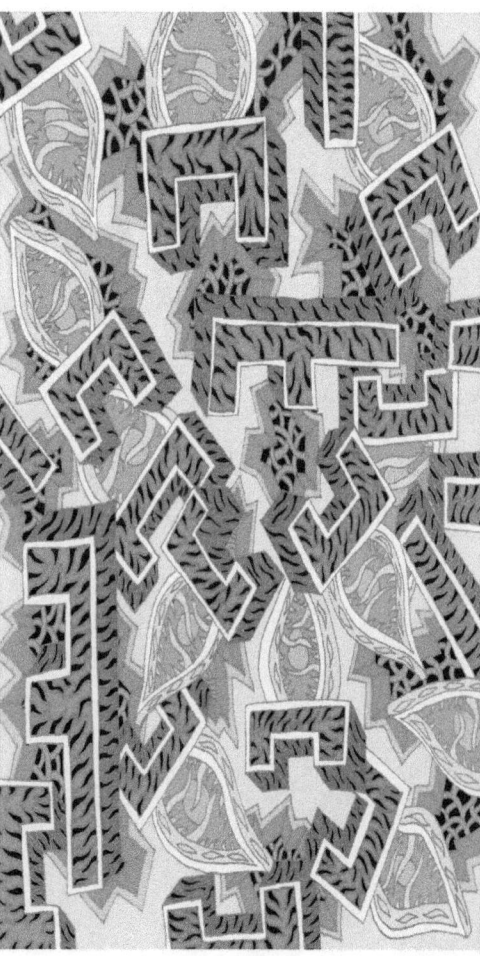

www.ingramcontent.com/pod-product-compliance
Lightning Source LLC
Chambersburg PA
CBHW080541190526
45169CB00007B/2591